Praise for *Transforming Schools for English Learners*

"School administrators, resource facilitators, and classroom teachers will find a wealth of strategies and research-based, comprehensive solutions for teaching English language learners. Whether a school district has a large population of English learners or is faced with designing an individualized program for just a few, this is a useful toolkit, at once theoretical and practical." —**Lynne T. Díaz-Rico, Professor of Education, California State University, San Bernardino**

"This book addresses issues that school administrators new to EL instruction need to know. Each chapter contains useful tools that deal with student assessment, placement, and monitoring." —**Margarita Calderón, Professor Emeritus, Johns Hopkins University, Baltimore, MD**

"This book is an excellent resource for school leaders who want to build an effective learning environment for English language learners. Zacarian covers a variety of topics including a summary of federal laws and how to select the right program model for your district, building an effective ESL program, establishing successful relationships with parents, designing content area lessons, and analyzing student performance. Written in a user-friendly style and based on current research, this is the book that every administrator and stakeholder should have." —**Judie Haynes, Author and President, New Jersey Teachers of English to Speakers of Other Languages/New Jersey Bilingual Educators, Union, NJ**

"Dr. Zacarian clearly and succinctly identifies the frequent misunderstandings and misconceptions that can occur between families of English language learners and teachers and administrators. She uses real-life experiences to illustrate the barriers faced by these families and offers effective solutions to help these students access college and to help schools integrate new immigrant families and students." —**Margaret O'Hare, Director, Massachusetts Parent Information and Resource Center (PIRC)**

"This book provides school leaders with clear and constructive guidance on how to reenvision schools with growing numbers of English learners. Debbie Zacarian addresses the questions of leaders who realize that schools that wish to succeed in the 21st century must rethink the organization, curriculum, analysis of data, assessments, and relations with families. The book is attentive to the theoretical underpinnings of second language acquisition as well as the day-to-day challenges facing school leaders." —**Eileen de los Reyes, Assistant Superintendent, Office of English Language Learners, Boston Public Schools**

"This book will help teachers formulate an appropriate program model by using effective data in tandem with parental support to enhance student success. District leaders will find it a valuable navigation tool for meeting the needs of English language learners." —**Sherry Gelinas, Director of Language Acquisition, Leominster Public Schools, MA**

Transforming
Schools
for English
Learners

Transforming Schools for English Learners

A Comprehensive Framework for School Leaders

Debbie Zacarian

CORWIN
A SAGE Company

CORWIN
A SAGE Company

FOR INFORMATION:

Corwin
A SAGE Company
2455 Teller Road
Thousand Oaks, California 91320
(800) 233-9936
Fax: (800) 417-2466
www.corwin.com

SAGE Ltd.
1 Oliver's Yard
55 City Road
London EC1Y 1SP
United Kingdom

SAGE India Pvt. Ltd.
B 1/I 1 Mohan Cooperative Industrial Area
Mathura Road, New Delhi 110 044
India

SAGE Asia-Pacific Pte. Ltd.
33 Pekin Street #02-01
Far East Square
Singapore 048763

Acquisitions Editor: Dan Alpert
Associate Editor: Megan Bedell
Editorial Assistant: Sarah Bartlett
Production Editor: Cassandra Margaret Seibel
Copy Editor: Sarah J. Duffy
Typesetter: C&M Digitals (P) Ltd.
Proofreader: Jenifer Kooiman
Indexer: Wendy Allex
Cover Designer: Karine Hovsepian
Permissions Editor: Karen Ehrmann

Printed in the United States of America.

Library of Congress Cataloging-in-Publication Data

Zacarian, Debbie.

Transforming schools for English learners: a comprehensive framework for school leaders/ Debbie Zacarian.

p. cm.
Includes bibliographical references and index.

ISBN 978-1-4129-9040-0 (pbk.)

1. English language—Study and teaching—United States—Foreign speakers. 2. School management and organization—United States. I. Title.

PE1128.A2Z33 2011
428.2'4071073—dc22
2010051779

This book is printed on acid-free paper.

11 12 13 14 15 10 9 8 7 6 5 4 3 2 1

Contents

Dedication and Acknowledgments

This book was written with the support of many people. Francis Bailey, Judie Haynes, Audrey Morse, Barbara Passo, Ken Pransky, and Barbara Rothenberg generously read early versions of the manuscript. Various administrators and teachers from Massachusetts' public and public charter schools and the Collaborative for Educational Services graciously opened their classrooms and school communities and shared their experiences working with culturally and linguistically diverse populations. In addition, Dan Alpert, Cassandra Seibel, and Sarah Duffy at Corwin greatly supported the publication of this manuscript.

Writing a book involves long hours, dedication, and passion. This would not have been possible without the encouragement of my husband, Matt.

The adage that it takes a village to raise a child speaks to the support that I received to "raise" *Transforming Schools for English Learners*.

PUBLISHER'S ACKNOWLEDGMENTS

Corwin gratefully acknowledges the contributions of the following reviewers:

David Bautista, Superintendent/Adjunct University Instructor/Visiting Instructor
Woodburn School District/Western Oregon University/University of Guadalajara
Woodburn, OR

Margarita Calderón, Professor Emerita
Johns Hopkins University
Washington, DC

Tracy Clark, Director I—English Language Learner Programs
Clark County School District
Las Vegas, NV

Bruce Clemmer, Director—English Language Learner Programs
Clark County School District
Las Vegas, NV

Maria Dove, Professor
Molloy College
Department of Education
Rockville Centre, NY

Andrea Honigsfeld, Professor and Associate Dean
Molloy College
Department of Education
Rockville Centre, NY

Barb Keating, Principal
Lord Kelvin Community School
New Westminster School District
New Westminster, BC
Canada

Beth Madison, Principal
George Middle School
Portland, OR

Teresa Vega-Iniguez, Educational Administrator
San Luis Obispo County Office of Education
San Luis Obispo, CA

Rosa M. Villarreal, Director—Bilingual/ESL/Prekindergarten
Round Rock Independent School District
Round Rock, TX

Carol Wertheimer, Literacy Consultant
Glen Head, NY

About the Author

Debbie Zacarian, EdD, is the director of the Center for English Language Education and the Center for Advancing Student Achievement at the Collaborative for Educational Services, in Northampton, Massachusetts. The two centers provide professional development, licensure programming, and consulting for educators of culturally and linguistically diverse populations. Debbie has written policies regarding English learners for many urban, suburban, and rural districts and been a consultant at the state level. She is the coauthor of *Teaching English Language Learners Across Content Areas,* a 2010 ASCD publication. Debbie was a columnist for TESOL's *Essential Teacher* publication throughout its tenure, writing about issues related to secondary education. Debbie holds a doctorate in educational policy and research from the University of Massachusetts at Amherst and was a clinical faculty lecturer there for over a decade, teaching courses in language policy, theories of language acquisition, assessment and evaluation, research on language acquisition, curriculum development for language and content learning, and educational administration. Debbie also created and was the director of the Amherst Public Schools English Language Education Program for over 20 years—a program that was noted as a state and national model. She was commended by the Massachusetts Department of Education for her work in multicultural education. Debbie has been an educational consultant at the local, state, and national levels in the areas of English language education, closing the achievement gap, special education as it relates to students from diverse populations, and educational leadership. Recognized as a leading authority, she served as a member of the Commissioner's Bilingual Advisory Committee for the Massachusetts Department of Education. She has delivered many papers and presentations at the state and national levels, including at the annual meetings of the American Educational Research Association and Teachers of English to Speakers of Other Languages.

Introduction

Travel to Prairietown School, a small elementary school in a rural region of our country. Until recently, its population consisted of English-speaking administrators, teachers, students, parents, and community members. While its educators have not changed, they have begun to notice a small number of English learners (ELs) enrolling in the school. Continue traveling to Oceanside School, a suburban coastal community that has about 50 Spanish-speaking ELs in its district. Educators there also are noticing a difference; the number of students who are ELs is increasing rapidly, as is the number of languages that they speak. Finally, travel to Bustle City, an urban high school. English-speaking students used to be its dominant population. Now, English learners are the majority, and a growing number have had significant interruptions to their education. These realities are greatly transforming schools in the United States (August, 2008; Calderón & Minaya-Rowe, 2010; Goldenberg & Coleman, 2010; Hollins & Guzman, 2005; Zehr, 2009).

School leaders and educators of preservice and inservice administrators and teachers are asking themselves and others how to create and implement or strengthen policies, decisions, and day-to-day operations for the benefit of this growing population. Sadly, many are learning that whether achievement is measured by the assessments that are required according to the No Child Left Behind Act or the National Report Card known as the National Assessment of Educational Progress, the outcome is not positive. Many students are failing, and the achievement gap between ELs and the total student population is significant and growing (Goldenberg & Coleman, 2010; Zehr, 2009).

Transforming Schools for English Learners focuses on the ways in which school leaders—including superintendents, principals, curriculum supervisors, teacher-leaders, teacher educators, and others—can create effective school policies, practices, and structures for ELs in their particular contexts. The goal of this book is to help administrators, policymakers, and stakeholders who are just beginning to work with ELs or are veterans to build a school environment where ELs can flourish. Each chapter opens with a scenario and focuses on a key element of English language education programming.

1

Chapter 1: Administering Schools With English Learners provides a description of this ever-expanding population of students, their educational programming, and their teachers. It presents an analysis about what the demographics tell us and a rationale for developing English language education programming that is targeted to the needs of individual districts.

Chapter 2: Developing a Rationale for Programming by Understanding Key Historical Events, Principles, and Program Model Types presents the major historical events that led to the current laws and regulations governing the education of ELs, key principles of second language acquisition, and a description of the various types of program models for teaching ELs.

Chapter 3: Selecting Effective Program Models discusses the process and protocols for identifying ELs, selecting a program model, staffing the model, and evaluating its effectiveness. Included in this chapter are forms and protocols associated with the various processes involved in the identification, program selection, and ongoing evaluation tasks and procedures.

Chapter 4: Designing, Implementing, and/or Strengthening the English as a Second Language Component describes the English language development component of an English language education program. It details the organizational structures, such as time allocation and staffing considerations, that should be included to effectively implement this critical component.

Chapter 5: Addressing the Subject Matter Component of an English Language Education Program highlights the fact that, as schools build, strengthen, and maintain programs for ELs, it is important to define what constitutes a high-quality content lesson and learning environment. This chapter provides eight guiding principles for providing such lessons for English language development and content learning and a checklist for teachers, peers, supervisors, and others to use in assessing the overall success of content planning and delivery.

Chapter 6: Emphasizing the Importance of Parent Engagement acknowledges that establishing relationships with parents and extended family members is an important objective for school leaders at all grade levels. Many teachers and administrators are not familiar with the various cultural norms of ELs and their families, and many parents of ELs are not familiar with American school practices. This chapter provides a four-pronged framework for creating strong parent-school partnerships.

Chapter 7: Identifying and Working With English Learners With Learning Differences and Learning Disabilities describes the nation's special education trends and the Individuals with Disabilities Education Act as it relates to ELs. It also delves into Response to Intervention and the factors that should be considered to use this framework effectively with ELs. The chapter offers a team approach for evaluating and improving the learning environment and outcomes for ELs and a protocol for engaging in this process.

Chapter 8: Making Data-Driven Decisions Based on Effective Measures of Student Performance discusses the complexities of fair and equitable assessment and evaluation of ELs and their programming. It provides a rationale for a four-pronged approach for addressing the particular socio-cultural, developmental, academic, and cognitive needs of students. It also offers a rationale for selecting and using a collaborative process for understanding ELs' academic performance and needs. Included in this chapter are protocols for examining the effectiveness of the classroom as well as school-parent engagement and community building.

REFERENCES

August, D. (2008). *Demographic overview.* In D. August & T. Shanahan (Eds.), *Developing reading and writing in second language learners: Lessons from the report of the National Literacy Panel on language-minority children and youth* (pp. 538–549). New York: Routledge.

Calderón, M. E., & Minaya-Rowe, L. (2010). *Preventing long-term ELs: Transforming schools to meet core standards.* Thousand Oaks, CA: Corwin.

Goldenberg, C., & Coleman, R. (2010). *Promoting academic achievement among English learners: A guide to the research.* Thousand Oaks, CA: Corwin.

Hollins, E. R., & Guzman, M. T. (2005). Research on preparing teachers for diverse populations. In M. Cochran-Smith & K. M. Zeichner (Eds.), *Studying teacher education: A report of the AERA panel on research and teacher education* (pp. 477–548). Mahwah, NJ: Lawrence Erlbaum.

Zehr, M. A. (2009, January 8). Adopted tongue: English language learners pose policy puzzle. *Education Week,* pp. 8–9.

1

Administering Schools With English Learners

Manuel moved to the United States from El Salvador when he was 13 years old. In El Salvador, he had worked on his uncle's bus as the ticket taker and money exchanger. He is a very sweet, polite Spanish speaker who came to the United States without any formal schooling or prior exposure to English. His family moved to Centerville, a small town, to work in a relative's restaurant, where they hoped they could earn a living wage. Although Manuel had no prior schooling, Mr. Pronowitz, the principal at Centerville Middle School, decided to place Manuel in the eighth grade so that he could be with his same-age peers.

Ernesto moved from Mexico to the same town as Manuel. His father, an engineer, had been transferred to work in a city near Centerville. Before moving, Ernesto had completed seventh grade in a private school where he had received an excellent education. He loved mathematics and had won an award for "most promising mathematician." When his parents enrolled him in Centerville Middle School, his father tried to convey Ernesto's prior schooling experiences to Mr. Pronowitz. But because his English was limited and his wife and Ernesto could not speak any English at all, Mr. Pronowitz could not understand much about Ernesto's strengths, achievements, and needs. He assigned him to the same grade as Manuel.

A few days after Manuel and Ernesto began school, they were given a standardized test to determine their fluency in English. Both scored at the beginning level. With this testing information, Mr. Pronowitz assigned them to the English as a second language (ESL) class that met for one 45-minute class period a day. He also placed them in the same remedial classes for the rest of their school day. He assumed that Manuel and Ernesto would feel more comfortable with each other because they were the school's only Spanish-speaking English learners (ELs). He also thought that placing them in remedial classes would be less demanding for them because they were both beginning learners of English, unlike the other ELs in the school. Overall, Mr. Pronowitz thought that these placements were academically appropriate and sensitive to the boys' needs.

When Manuel and Ernesto began speaking to each other, Ernesto quickly realized that Manuel had never been to school. Ernesto also felt that his classes, especially math, were much easier than he was used to. He assumed that being a Spanish-speaking EL in the United States must mean that he was not a smart or good student. He felt isolated and divorced from everything that was familiar to him. Within a few weeks, he began to feel very depressed. By the end of the first term, Ernesto had decided to stop attending school. His parents quickly moved him to a parochial school, assuming that it would be a much better place for their son than Centerville Middle School was. When Mr. Pronowitz was made aware of Ernesto's absences, he called Ernesto's home. He was unable to communicate with Ernesto or his parents. While he thought about Ernesto occasionally, he never knew why he missed so much school. When Ernesto stopped attending altogether, Mr. Pronowitz assumed that he had moved to another town.

Manuel also felt entirely lost. He could not understand any of his classes. They were moving much too quickly for him. He was constantly exhausted from trying to learn. At least Ernesto could help him understand a little about what was happening. But when Ernesto was absent, which had become a frequent occurrence, Manuel's day was hopelessly confusing. He began thinking about quitting school. After a month of struggling, he decided to meet with Mr. Pronowitz. He was failing all of his classes and desperately wanted to do well. He asked his uncle if he would come to translate for him at the meeting. When they met, Mr. Pronowitz decided that Manuel should be referred for a special education evaluation to see if he had a learning disability. With Manuel's parents' approval (they trusted the school and didn't believe it was their place to do anything more than listen and heed the principal's advice), the referral process began. The assessors assumed that Manuel's poor progress was due to a disability as opposed to what it really was: lack of a formal prior education and academic skills, even in his first language.

Sergi, a Ukrainian-American EL who was born in the United States and attended Centerville Middle School for three years, then moved to New York City, where he enrolled in the ninth grade. He was one of the city's 148,000 ELs (Zehr, 2009), and when his English proficiency was tested, Sergi was found to be at the fourth of five English proficiency levels. The school decided that he did not need to be enrolled in the English language education program. Within the first few weeks, Sergi was unable to keep up with his peers. He had trouble grasping some of the vocabulary and course assignments and tasks. He pored over his homework and stayed up well after midnight each night. He attempted to go for afterschool help but worried that he would be fired from the afterschool job that his family depended on. As a result, Sergi began failing many of his courses and thinking that school was not for him. By the end of the ninth grade, Sergi was like the other 41.8% of the city's ELs—a dropout. According to Zehr, less than a quarter of New York City's ELs graduate within four years, and the overall dropout rate of 41.8% continues.

These scenarios are not that unusual among our nation's ELs. Many are failing, being referred to special education programs, and dropping out of school. Whether we measure achievement by the tests that each state administers to its students, as required by the federal No Child Left Behind Act, or by the national report card known as the National Assessment of Educational Progress, the achievement gap between the nation's ELs and the total student population is significant and growing (Zehr, 2009). On the National Report Card, as noted by Ballantyne, Sanderman, and Levy (2008), ELs had a score of 38.2% in reading versus the general population's score of 70.5%, and only 43.8% of ELs scored proficient in mathematics assessments versus 67.4% for all students.

These outcomes speak to not only the need to think of more responsive ways for designing programming, but also the ways in which we lead schools that ELs attend. This book focuses on school leadership for the purpose of creating and sustaining effective programs for ELs. It is intended for school- and district-level leaders who are charged with administering and supervising the curriculum, instructional programming, teachers and support staff, parent and community outreach and engagement, and all related activities regarding the education of ELs.

The following questions are intended to help us in this reexamination process:

- Who are ELs?
- Typically, who are the teachers of ELs?
- How does what we are doing complement our district's and school's mission and vision?

WHO ARE ELs?

ELs represent a large and growing population in our nation's schools. Between 1995 and 2005, the number of the nation's ELs grew by 57%. During the same time period, growth in the number of all students was flat. Urban schools, which were once dominated by American monolingual speakers of English, have rapidly shifted to being much more linguistically diverse. Simultaneously, suburban and rural districts that had never had ELs were beginning to have them. In 1992, there were between 1.2 and 1.7 million ELs in public school (Nieto, 1992). By 2005, that population had jumped to 5.1 million (Maxwell, 2009). By 2009, they were at least 10% of the nation's K–12 students (García, Jensen, & Scribner, 2009), and some believed that the actual percentage was much higher (Capps et al., 2005). Further, while most ELs are concentrated in California, Florida, Illinois, New Jersey, New York, and Texas (Capps et al., 2005), the National Center for Education Statistics (2004) indicates that over 50% of ELs attend schools in places where they account for less than 1% of the student population. The remaining half attend schools with very large populations of ELs, nearly 30%, and are often isolated from the general population (Capps et al., 2005). These realities have deep implications for the choices that school leaders make on behalf of the ELs in their schools, including the reality that some will lead schools with small numbers of ELs and others large.

It is important to understand that ELs are not a monolithic group. They represent 350 different language groups (García et al., 2009). And while the majority (68%) are Latino, 14% are non-Hispanic white, 13% are Asian/Pacific Islander, 4% are Black, and 1% are classified as "other." Altogether, 200 countries are represented among the nation's ELs, but many ELs are born in United States ("A Distinct Population," 2009). Some schools have ELs from a wide range of language groups, while others have students from just one. Even neighboring schools may have very different languages represented among their ELs.

The primary language that a student speaks is but one descriptor. Even students who speak Spanish, for example, have distinct cultures and represent many countries. Some hail from countries in Central and South America, others are from Caribbean nations, and many others were born in the United States. They also speak different dialects. The same diversity is true for students from any language group.

There are also other factors that are important to consider. Some of the nation's ELs have rich literacy and prior schooling experiences (New Levine & McCloskey, 2009; Pransky, 2008). Typically, these students' parents and families have strong literacy backgrounds. Books are commonplace in their homes, and parenting practices are oriented to developing the language and cognitive skills that their children will need in school. It is typical in these homes to observe parents reading a variety of texts and for their children to observe these literacy behaviors as part of their development. These students' home life resonates with everyday school practices such as doing homework and reading for pleasure. Thus, one segment of ELs enters school with strong, school-matched language and thinking skills as well as an understanding about formal schooling. However, this does not negate that they initially need cultural sensitivity so as not to feel alienated from the school culture as well as language support to address their need to learn academic content and English.

Conversely, there is also a large group of non-literacy-oriented ELs (Pransky, 2008). Typically, their families are less educated than those from literacy-oriented homes, and parenting practices are not oriented to American public school practices. This is not to say that all parents do not love and nurture their children. It is to say that among the population of ELs, there are distinct groups, and one of these is not as well prepared for American public schools as the other. While these less-prepared ELs share the need for cultural sensitivity and language support, they also need an educational program that emphasizes their need to develop school-matched thinking and language skills (Pransky, 2008).

There is also a large number of ELs who have experienced major disruptions in their families' lives, such as poverty, war, long-term stress, and other factors. Because of these disruptions, they have not had the systematic acculturation experiences of either the literacy- or non-literacy-oriented communities. When they enroll in American schools, it may be their first exposure to literacy and content learning (Calderón, 2007). They have not had the opportunity in either home or school to develop the skills that they need in order to learn. This population of ELs poses particularly distinct challenges to educators.

Poverty is also a big concern for many of our nation's ELs: Close to 66% come from families whose income is 200% below the poverty level ("A Distinct Population," 2009; Goldenberg & Coleman, 2010). Students who are learning English are among the very poorest of students in our schools.

Each of these factors is important to consider when leading programs for ELs. While many of us are most concerned with the speed at which students will learn English and are often impatient with the process, the variation among our nation's ELs must not be ignored, as it will greatly help us in creating and sustaining programs that work.

In sum, the nation's ELs come from a wide range of personal, linguistic, cultural, educational, and socioeconomic backgrounds. This population continues to grow at a significant rate as a percentage of our nation's students. Overall, they are performing at a much lower rate than their English-speaking peers. And these realities are occurring against a backdrop of schools whose teachers and administrators feel unprepared for them (Maxwell, 2009).

To advocate for the best program and to support their teachers, school leaders need to understand their EL populations very well, from a cultural and linguistic perspective. They also need to understand that students come from diverse backgrounds and have varying degrees of school readiness. Finally, they need to learn specifically about the effects of poverty on learning and how to help students overcome these effects.

Are there commonalities among the ways in which we organize programming for ELs?

If you were to visit classrooms in the United States that have ELs, you might notice many different features. In some, you would hear the student's native language being spoken. In others, you would hear only English; even using another language informally is discouraged. You might also observe students having little to no support to learn English in some schools, while in others you would observe ELs in multigrade classrooms spending the school day with other ELs. You might travel only a few miles to another school and see students spending half of their school day learning in one language and half in another. There are literally hundreds of programming models for ELs to learn English as they learn academic content (Goldenberg & Coleman, 2010; Soltero, 2004). While many believe that the name of a program, such as *transitional bilingual education*, defines the how it is practiced, the reality is that each program model can be enacted differently in one district than it is in the next, adding up to the hundreds of types (Lessow-Hurley, 2008). We will look more closely at these in the next chapter.

School leaders have to sift through each of these types to try to identify the one that they believe will work the most effectively in their context. They also have to consider how prepared their school's or district's teachers are to work with ELs.

TYPICALLY, WHO ARE THE TEACHERS OF ELs?

In 1992, most of the nation's teachers were White, middle-class, monolingual English speakers (Zeichner & Hoeft, 1996), and the situation has not changed dramatically since then (Hollins & Guzman, 2005). Teacher preparation programs are heavily dominated by "white middle class females, from suburbs and small towns and have limited experience with people from cultures other than their own" (Hollins & Guzman, 2005, p. 485). Not surprisingly, in an empirical review of 101 studies that were conducted between 1980 and 2002 to investigate teacher preparation to work with students from diverse populations, Hollins and Guzman found that most students enrolled in teacher preparation programs were more comfortable and preferred working with students and parents from experiences similar to their own. Courses in key areas that are needed for teaching ELs, such as bilingual education, second language acquisition, and multicultural education, were more likely to be optional electives (Ladson-Billings, 1995).

Most of the nation's teachers have no training or experience working with the growing population of ELs. They are not sure how to address these students' English language learning needs or how to adapt subject matter instruction for them. Because many teachers have no experience working with students unlike themselves—including students who live in poverty and older students who have very limited literacy skills, or none at all, and no prior formal schooling—they have no experiential framework to draw from. All of these factors pose complex challenges for educators.

Unfortunately, federal law does not require teachers to be highly qualified to teach ELs (Honawar, 2009). What is equally concerning is that training to teach American public school ELs, particularly for general education teachers who spend a good deal of time with ELs, is not required in most states ("A Distinct Population," 2009). This contributes to why there are few commonalities among our nation's states in terms of teaching ELs (Honawar, 2009). At the same time, while training seems like an obvious solution, it is extraordinarily challenging to keep pace with the growth of the EL population and wide variety of their needs. According to the EPE Research Center (2009a), 56,000 ESL teachers will be needed during the next five years. This number is staggering when you consider that there are not enough as it is and it doesn't include the content teachers needed. If all these numbers are factored into the equation, it is likely that *most* of the nation's teachers lack training in how to work successfully with ELs. Just as ELs must often sink or swim in the educational system, teachers are expected by their school leaders—who, like them, are not trained to know better—to sink or swim in teaching ELs. The poor performance of ELs seems to parallel the lack of preparation among their teachers to teach them.

School leaders need to try to ensure that the teachers who work with ELs in their school—classroom/content teachers and ESL teachers alike—are well trained.

What about teachers who have had training?

Some schools do have general education teachers who are trained to teach ELs. Many are members of the same language minority groups as their students and have a solid understanding about their students' language, culture, and prior schooling. They have been trained in the theories and practices of second language acquisition and understand the process of learning a new language and teaching their students. Others, most commonly ESL teachers, also have been trained to teach English to ELs, understand the developmental process of learning a new language, and are prepared to teach their students.

Sadly, while these teachers have knowledge that many of their colleagues lack, a significant percentage report feeling marginalized by their colleagues (Cummins, 2001; Zacarian, 2007). Rather than being valued as assets, they all too frequently feel relegated to the fringes of the school.

They believe that their schools are enacting what is occurring to linguistic minorities in the world around them, namely, they are not considered members of their school communities and are often treated as inferior and powerless by their peers (Cummins, 1994, 2001; Zacarian, 2007).

Luckily, some teachers who have been trained to work with ELs are not marginalized, feel empowered as leaders of their schools, and are valued as assets for teaching ELs. This is particularly true for a large group of teachers who participated in a longitudinal study that led to what is known as the *sheltered instruction observation protocol* (Echevarria, Vogt, & Short, 2008). In this study, researchers from the Center for Applied Linguistics and the Center for Research on Equity and Diversity looked at schools in which ELs were performing well. They observed classroom teachers of ELs for a five-year period and noted the elements for planning and delivering an effective lesson. From this research, they developed an observational protocol that highlighted the elements that the researchers believe are essential for students at the third, fourth, and final stage of English language learning. At the heart of this research is a strong belief in collaboration among teachers.

We need to understand ways for leading our schools so that ELs can succeed in the learning process and become active members of their school community. School leaders have an enormous, if not the most essential, role in the educational programming for the nation's ELs. They are the primary architects and supervisors of the instructional programming that is provided. Knowing that it is not likely that teachers will have been trained in this important area, that they may be uncomfortable working with students from backgrounds other than their own, and that they may, intentionally or unintentionally, marginalize teachers who are EL student advocates and who have had appropriate training and experience, leaders must seek ways to build and sustain effective programming.

HOW DOES WHAT WE ARE DOING COMPLEMENT OUR DISTRICT'S AND SCHOOL'S MISSION AND VISION?

Many if not most schools have a mission statement. Mission statements typically mean that leaders have examined their school and its core purpose to define and make available to the community their school's or district's goals and the ways in which they will be measured. Mission statements might be considered the symbolic heart of the school, as they describe the best of an organization's core values and beliefs for building a school culture and climate. In mission statements, school leaders often encapsulate what they believe to be important for learners and the school community.

The same type of process is needed for creating a program for ELs. Doing so takes time, collaboration, and a belief that the program must complement the mission of the school while also addressing the complex needs of language-minority students. Selecting a one-size-fits-all model does not work for the widely diverse population of ELs.

To create an optimal English language education program, whether for large or small number of ELs, requires that we think of learners as individuals, members of the school community, and members of the town or city community as well. To lead our schools, we must collaborate with our students, their families, teachers, and other stakeholders.

In Chapter 2, we will begin to look more closely at developing a rationale for a district's or school's English language education program model for its ELs.

REFERENCES

A distinct population. (2009). *Quality Counts, 28*(17), 15.

Ballantyne, K. G., Sanderman, A. R., Levy, J. (2008). *Educating English language learners: Building teacher capacity.* Washington, DC: National Clearinghouse for English Language Acquisition.

Calderón, M. (2007). *Teaching reading to English language learners, Grades 6–12.* Thousand Oaks, CA: Corwin.

Capps, R., Fix, M., Murray, J., Ost, J., Passel, J., & Herwantoro, S. (2005). *The new demography of America's schools: Immigration and the No Child Left Behind Act.* Washington, DC: Urban Institute.

Cummins, J. (1994). Knowledge, power, and identity in teaching English as a second language. In F. Genesee (Ed.), *Educating second language children: The whole child, the whole curriculum, the whole community* (pp. 33–58). New York: Cambridge University Press.

Cummins, J. (2001). *Language, power, and pedagogy: Bilingual children in the crossfire.* Bristol, UK: Multilingual Matters.

Echevarria, J., Vogt, M. J., Short, D. J. (2008). Making content comprehensible for English learners: The SIOP model (3rd ed.). Boston: Allyn & Bacon.

EPE Research Center. (2009a). *Perspectives on a population: English-language learners in American schools.* Bethesda, MD: Editorial Projects in Education.

García, E. E., Jensen, B. T., & Scribner, K. P. (April 2009). The demographic imperative. *Educational Leadership, 66*(7), 8–13.

Goldenberg, C., & Coleman, R. (2010). *Promoting academic achievement among English learners: A guide to the research.* Thousand Oaks: Corwin.

Hollins, E., & Guzman, M. T. (2005). Research on preparing teachers for diverse populations. In M. Cochran Smith & K. Zeichner (Eds.), *Studying teacher education: The report of the AERA panel on research and teacher education* (pp. 477–548). Mahwah, NJ: Lawrence Erlbaum.

Honawar, V. (2009). Training gets boost. *Quality Counts, 28*(17). Retrieved December 8, 2010, from http://www.edweek.org/ew/articles/2009/01/08/17training.h28.html

Ladson-Billings, G. (1995). Multicultural teacher education: Research, practice, and policy. In J. A. Banks & C. A. Banks (Eds.), *Handbook of research on multicultural education* (pp. 747–761). New York: Macmillan.

Lessow-Hurley, J. (2008). Foundations of dual language instruction (5th ed.). Boston: Allyn & Bacon.

Maxwell, L. A. (2009). Immigration transforms communities. *Quality Counts, 28*(17), 10–11.

National Center for Education Statistics. (2004). *English language learners in U.S. public schools: 1994 and 2000.* Retrieved December 10, 2010, from http://nces .ed.gov/pubsearch/pubsinfo.asp?pubid=2004035

New Levine, L., & McCloskey, M. (2009). *Teaching learners of English in mainstream classrooms K-8: One class, many paths.* New York: Pearson.

Nieto, S. (1992). *Affirming diversity: The sociopolitical context of multicultural education.* New York: Longman.

Pransky, K. (2008). *Beneath the surface: The hidden realities of teaching linguistically and culturally diverse young learners K–5.* Portsmouth, NH: Heinemann.

Soltero, S. (2004). *Dual language: Teaching and learning in two languages.* New York: Pearson.

Zacarian, D. (2007). Mascot or member? *Essential Teacher, 4*(3), 10–11.

Zehr, M. A. (2009). Adopted tongue: English language learners pose policy puzzle. *Quality Counts, 28*(17), 8–9.

Zeichner, K., & Hoeft, K. (1996). Teacher socialization for cultural diversity. In J. Sikula, T. Buttery, & E. Guyton (Eds.), *Handbook on research on teacher education* (2nd ed., pp. 525–547). New York: Macmillan.

2

Developing a Rationale for Programming by Understanding Key Historical Events, Principles, and Program Model Types

W hen Olivier moved from Cape Verde to Massachusetts, his mother enrolled him in a neighborhood school with the help of a relative who could speak English. The school's guidance counselor welcomed Olivier and his family and provided him with a class schedule. The schedule did not include anything to address his lack of English. Rather, it was the same one that his English-fluent peers received. It was felt that Olivier should be treated like everyone else. By the end of the first week, both Olivier and his teachers were very frustrated. The teachers weren't sure how to teach him because they couldn't communicate with him, and he was totally lost. What should or could the school have done?

Actually, it is required by federal law that students be identified as to whether or not they are English learners (ELs; U.S. Department of Education, Office of Civil Rights, 2000). Additional regulations require that when ELs are identified, they must be placed in programming that is known to be sound, with resources that are effective, that the programming be proven to be effective, and that adjustments be made when it isn't (U.S. Department of Education, Office of Civil Rights, 2005). The history behind these regulations provides important information for school leaders who need to institute programming for ELs. An examination of the following issues forms an important backdrop against which to answer the specific question about Olivier's school:

- What were the key historical events that led to the laws and regulations governing the education of ELs?
- What are the key principles of second language acquisition?
- What are the various models for English language education programming?

WHAT WERE THE KEY HISTORICAL EVENTS THAT LED TO THE LAWS AND REGULATIONS GOVERNING THE EDUCATION OF ELs?

The regulations governing the education of ELs are an outcome of major historical events. Some of these involved judicial decisions made by the U.S. Supreme Court, and others were formed in the court of public opinion. The civil rights movement of the 1960s led to many actions involving the rights of ELs (Reese, 2005). Prior to the 1960s, the right to an equal education was interpreted to mean that all students, regardless of their proficiency in English, were treated equally when they attended the same classrooms as their peers, or classrooms like their peers, and when instruction was delivered using the same books and curriculum. This practice was challenged during the civil rights movement when the country began to look more carefully at some of its discriminatory practices, including the education of its ELs (Reese, 2005).

In 1964, the Civil Rights Act was enacted. It states that any institution that receives federal funding cannot deny access to anyone to any program or activity based on their race, color, or national origin (U.S. Department of Justice, Office of Civil Rights, 2003). Then, in 1968, the same year in which Martin Luther King Jr. delivered the renowned "I have a dream" speech on the steps of the Lincoln Memorial, the Elementary and Secondary Education Act was amended to include the Bilingual Education Act. This was the first federal statute that addressed the particular learning needs of language-minority students (Baker, 2006; Osorio-O'Dea, 2001). Some believe that it was the result of a political movement intended to attract the Latino vote, while others claim that it was a genuine attempt to remedy the high failure rates among the nation's ELs (Crawford, 1996). Regardless, it marked the first time that the rights of ELs were brought into focus. Unfortunately, it did not lead to many changes as it failed to include specific regulations other than the general notion that schools could use innovative programming in the native language to teach English to the nation's students (Crawford, 1996; Reese, 2005). However, it did pave the way for schools to implement programming that allowed students to learn in their native language while they were learning English and led to what is now known as bilingual education.

According to the National Association of Bilingual Education (2009), the term *bilingual education* refers to "approaches in the classroom that use the native languages of English language learners (ELLs) for instruction" (para. 2). Further, it cites seven primary goals for bilingual education:

- teaching English
- fostering academic achievement
- acculturating immigrants to a new society
- preserving a minority group's linguistic and cultural heritage
- enabling English speakers to learn a second language
- developing national language resources
- or any combination of the above (para. 2)

Many federal regulations about ELs are a result of lawsuits filed in local courts across the country and appealed all the way to the Supreme Court. In *Lau v. Nichols,* for example, the Supreme Court ruled that schools must provide programming to help students overcome barriers to learning English. The definition of an EL became commonly known as a student who is not able to perform ordinary class work in English. Table 2.1 highlights six of the major Supreme Court cases. The ones that are shaded are considered to be the most seminal.

Each of the rulings in Table 2.1 should provide important safeguards for students so that they can receive a quality education. In sum, they require schools to identify ELs, provide research-based programming that is known to be sound, use adequate commitment and resources, evaluate the effectiveness of the programming, and make necessary changes using sound research-based models that are known to be effective to ensure that students learn English and content successfully. However, as seen in Chapter 1, many of the issues that led to these court cases have not been remedied.

Some believe that persisting disparities are a result of continued prejudice and discrimination toward the nation's language-minority population (Cummins, 2000). Without question, politics has continued to strongly affect language policies. Four states (California, Arizona, Colorado, and Massachusetts) have run ballot initiatives to restrict or eliminate bilingual education. Proponents of these initiatives argue that bilingual education is a failure and a reflection of the wrong language policies

Table 2.1 U. S. Supreme Court Cases Related to English Learners

Year	Name	Description of Case	Ruling
1973	Keyes v. Denver School District	The first de facto segregation case heard in the United States, arguing that particular groups of students (Latinos and Blacks) were largely separated from their peers.	Districts must desegregate their students (Horn & Kurlaender, 2006).
1974	Lau v. Nichols	Lau argued that the district was not providing an adequate education to its ELs because they could not sufficiently comprehend English.	Districts must take the steps needed to provide ELs with an instructional program in which they can perform ordinary class work in English. One year later (1975), the U.S. Secretary of Education issued the Lau Remedies, providing districts with guidelines for identifying and working with ELs (Crawford, 1996).
1974	Serna v. Portales	Latino plaintiffs claimed that their school district had ignored the English language and learning needs of their children. They believed that their children's rights to equal protection and equal educational opportunity were being denied.	District must do the following when there are a substantial number of ELs from the same language group: 1. expand bilingual bicultural instruction 2. measure student achievement 3. recruit and employ bilingual personnel (Crawford, 1996)
1975	Aspira v. Board of Education of the City of New York	This case argued that students who spoke little English were forced to attend schools in which instruction was offered primarily in English and that the results of this practice were inadequate	Districts must provide intensive instruction for students to learn English and can provide bilingual education in content areas when it is needed and reinforces students' use of their

Year	Name	Description of Case	Ruling
		programming, higher rates of underachievement and dropping out, and a much lower rate of economic opportunity compared with English-fluent peers.	primary language. Students must not be isolated or separated from their peers.
1978	Cintron v. Brentwood Union Free School District	This case argued that children were being segregated and isolated from their English-fluent peers.	Districts must provide methods for identifying and assessing ELs and transferring them into general education English classrooms using a method that does not segregate students (Dunklee & Shoop, 2006; Mid-Atlantic Equity Consortium, 1995).
1978	Castañeda v. Pickard	The district was segregating children based on their race and ethnicity, and had failed to implement a successful bilingual education program in which children would learn English.	Districts must establish a three-pronged test for ensuring that their educational program for ELs is consistent with a student's right to an education. It established that programming should be 1. based on sound educational research; 2. implemented with adequate commitment and resources; and 3. evaluated for its effectiveness, after a period of time, and that alternative research-based programming be sought if found not to be effective.

(Mendoza & Ayala, 1999; Montero & Chavez, 2001; Tamayo, Porter, & Rossell, 2001; Unz & Tuchman, 1997). They also claim that it is too expensive, and they promote an English-only ideology and an unfounded belief that English could be learned in a year (Crawford, 1996; Gonzalez, 2000). Arizona, California, and Massachusetts voted for the ballot initiatives to repeal bilingual education entirely. Years after the resulting policies went into effect, research was conducted to assess their outcome. Were students doing any better? The results did not show the significant improvements that the proponents had promised, and the achievement gap between ELs and their English-fluent peers continued (American Institutes for Research & WestEd, 2002; Burdick-Will & Gomez, 2006; Uriarte & Karp, 2009). As we saw in Chapter 1, ELs across the nation—whether the states they live in have or have not passed or repealed bilingual education laws—continue to perform much more poorly than their English-fluent peers.

While these anti-bilingual-education initiatives were occurring, in 2002 President Bush signed the No Child Left Behind Act (NCLB) into law with the intent of improving student achievement (U.S. Department of Education, 2002). The new law replaced the Elementary and Secondary Education Act, including the Bilingual Education Act, set new standards for the ways in which schools used federal funds, and set achievement standards for schools and students. It included four principles:

1. Stronger accountability for results

2. Greater flexibility among the nation's states, school districts, and schools in the use of federal funds

3. More choices for parents from disadvantaged backgrounds

4. An emphasis on teaching methods that have been proven to work (U.S. Department of Education, 2002)

New standards were also set to improve the achievement gaps between ELs and fluent speakers of English because "a congressionally mandated study found that these students [ELs] receive lower grades, are judged by their teachers to have lower academic abilities, and score below their classmates on standardized tests of reading and math" (U.S. Department of Education, 2002, p. 91). Under NCLB, federally funded schools with ELs were to focus on using what had been found to be successful practices for teaching ELs. To do this, it required

- teachers to be certified as English language proficient and proficient in the languages in which a program model is taught,
- using curriculum that is scientifically based and proven to be effective,
- states to have flexibility in choosing the teaching method for teaching ELs, and
- that 95% of the Title III funds used at the local level be used to teach ELs.

NCLB also placed a heavy emphasis on student performance:

- It established annual achievement objectives for ELs based on a set of standards and benchmarks for raising the English proficiency levels of ELs.
- It required annual assessments of students in English language arts and reading.
- It required states to ensure that their districts and schools were making measurable annual achievement objectives.

Additionally, NCLB required school districts to inform parents about the programming that was specifically targeted for teaching their children English, and it gave parents the right to choose among different program models, if more than one was available, as well as the right to remove their children from a program.

School leaders need to know and adhere to the federal laws regarding the education of ELs. Whether we lead English language education programming in Alaska or Florida, these laws provide us with a broad set of guidelines for creating and maintaining effective programming. Returning to the case presented in the opening of this chapter, had Olivier's school principal adhered to these guidelines, he would have taken steps to provide Olivier with sound programming and the needed resources. He would also have instituted a process by which the program could be examined to ensure that it was working, or change it as needed.

Another important step for understanding how to put the regulations into practice is to understand some of the key principles of second language acquisition, including the major research studies that have focused on ELs. They provide us with important information about the various program models for leading schools with ELs.

WHAT ARE THE KEY PRINCIPLES OF SECOND LANGUAGE ACQUISITION?

Jim Cummins has contributed greatly to what we understand the principles of second language acquisition to be. To communicate effectively in social situations, Cummins and Swain (1986) states that we must have the *basic interpersonal communication skills* (BICS) to interact with others. He claims that this takes a much shorter time (one to three years to attain native-speaker proficiency) than it does to learn the language we use to express the higher-order thinking skills that we need for academic learning. A very common example of the impact of academic versus social language would be the student who can speak in English easily with peers on the school bus but cannot perform grade-level academic tasks in English in the classroom. Teachers and administrators may well wonder whether such a student is lazy in class or has some learning disability. Actually, that student is merely working his way through a very predictable process and timetable of second language learning.

Using language socially is different than using it for academic purposes

Using language with peers on the playground, at lunch, on the school bus, or in play after school is quite different than using language in academic contexts. One reason is because social situations are often supported by a context, physical cues such as facial gestures and body movements, and the environment in which the situation is taking place. Consider a second language learner playing jump rope at recess. She can participate actively in the event by observing and imitating her peers. Because her friends' language use is so contextual, the words they use during this play event are clear and relatively simple, and their sentence structures are probably simple as well. The event facilitates the student's ability to communicate while playing and to quickly take ownership of some of the language.

In contrast, the language used in an academic setting is more implicit and abstract, more complex, and less reliant on context and interpersonal cues. For example, let's say that the kids playing jump rope have returned to class from recess and are engaged in a science lesson about mammals. While there are some pictures, there is a lot of reading as well as lists of attributes. Language use quickly moves from the social event at recess to a context in which there are far fewer contextual cues. Students are required to use complex and specialized language and language structures to listen, speak, read, write, and learn. Certain background knowledge about mammals is also needed.

Cummins refers to academic language development as *cognitive academic language proficiency* (CALP; Cummins & Swain, 1986). Academic success requires the development of communicative skills (listening speaking, reading, and writing) in the content area (e.g., math, science, social studies) along with the much-needed "content knowledge, use of higher-order thinking skills, and mastery of basic academic skills" (Goldenberg & Coleman, 2010, p. 83). Research shows that developing these CALP skills takes time-intensive instruction, and it is a developmental process (August & Shanahan, 2006, 2008; Collier & Thomas, 1989, 2002; Cummins, 1981; Goldenberg & Coleman, 2010). While the terms *BICS* and *CALP* have been replaced with "informal less demanding conversational language and the more formal generally more demanding academic language necessary for school success" (Goldenberg & Coleman, 2010, p. 62), the two are not mutually exclusive, nor is it really one versus the other. Rather, as important as it is for students to develop oral language skills, educational success depends on students' mastery of academic language.

The professional organization Teachers of English to Speakers of Other Languages (TESOL; 2006) has worked with several states to produce standards to assist educators who teach ELs. The standards consider the developmental stages involved in acquiring BICS and CALP or social and academic language and are organized around three important premises:

1. Language learning is a developmental process and, as such, should be separated into grade levels.

2. It involves three goals: to use English for social purposes, to use English for academic purposes, and to use English in socially and culturally appropriate ways (TESOL's ESL Standards).

3. Some ELs will enter American public and public charter schools with little to no formal prior education, which will require school leaders to address the particular nonliteracy orientations of their students in order to provide effective programming.

Students from literacy-oriented, non-literacy-oriented, and culturally disrupted backgrounds

Some students come from homes and communities where literacy practices are present, as is an understanding about school expectations. These are not just book-related practices. Children from these communities develop certain cultural (e.g., independence in learning), linguistic (e.g., high vocabularies), and cognitive (e.g., metacognition) skills through their home and community interactions when they are young that privilege them later in a school setting.

Other ELs come from homes where there are far fewer literacy practices and where the orientation is not geared toward school. They are not denied the above skills forever, but are on a different timeline in developing them. There are many reasons why some students come from non-literacy-oriented homes. Some may live in communities where literacy is not needed or encouraged. Many times, the parents themselves are not well educated. School leaders must be on guard so that children from nonliteracy orientations are not overreferred to special education just because their academic progress is slower.

A third possibility exists: children who experience circumstances of cultural disruption. Children may have experienced a significant amount of upheaval in their lives, or the cultural cohesiveness of their upbringing has been disrupted. Sometimes disruption can result in interrupted schooling (especially for older learners coming from abroad). In addition, a large number of EL families who live in poverty have experienced great turmoil, such as war, and significant long-term family stress. These circumstances interrupt the community's culturally appropriate interactions with parents, whether the children are from literacy-oriented or non-literacy-oriented communities. Because of the variety of circumstances that bring many immigrants and refugees to this country, students who come from non-literacy-oriented and culturally disrupted homes and communities represent a significant portion of the nation's ELs. They usually take much longer to develop CALP skills than do children who experience culturally cohesive literacy-oriented upbringing (Pransky, 2008).

How long does it take to learn a second language?

School leaders must have a good understanding about the time and the conditions that are needed to learn a second language well enough to be able to perform ordinary class work in English, both for BICS and especially for CALP development. All ELs must be given sufficient time to develop CALP skills, and their programming must be designed for this purpose. For literacy-oriented ELs, it will take less time and teachers mostly just need to skillfully support a process that students will naturally be engaged in doing. For non-literacy-oriented and culturally disrupted ELs, the process not only will be longer, but it must be made more explicit and be directly taught.

Two major government-funded reviews of research (August & Shanahan, 2006; Genesee, Lindholm-Leary, Saunders, & Christian, 2006) provide the most comprehensive and up-to-date findings about the education of language-minority students (Goldenberg & Coleman, 2010). These studies found that it takes one to three years to become conversationally fluent and four to six years or more to achieve a Level 4 on a five-point scale of proficiency in English. Further, such progress may not be directly related to how fluent a student is in social conversational situations (Goldenberg & Coleman, 2010). For example, a student's capacity to engage in a social conversation about the previous night's school basketball game is not an indicator of his capacity to engage successfully in an academic context. Developing academic proficiency in English is a long process, and each stage is not the same in terms of the length of time that it takes to move from one to another. Drawing from the two government-funded research reviews about second language learning, Goldenberg and Coleman (2010) found that "progress was slower between level 3 and advanced levels 4 and 5" (p. 69). One of the most important factors regarding the length of time that it takes is whether a student is from a literacy-oriented or non-literacy-oriented home.

Virginia Collier and Wayne Thomas (1989) have examined the length of time that it takes for ELs to become "proficient in English," a phrase that, under the federal law, means able to perform ordinary class work in English. They conducted a longitudinal 10-year study of 2,000 students in a large urban school district that was fairly affluent and literacy oriented. Their goal was to find out how long it took beginning learners of English to reach native performance in English at the 50th percentile on norm-referenced tests (i.e., the ability to perform ordinary class work in English).

For their study, Collier and Thomas (1989) selected ELs whose academic achievement scores in their native language were at or above grade level. They selected this high-achieving group of students, as they believed that they would learn English the fastest and that the results would provide key information about learners at the high end of the spectrum. They also selected students who had the same program model for learning English: instruction in English as a second language (ESL) on a pull-out basis. No support in the native language was provided, and students did not receive content support in ESL.

The students were first given two years' time to learn English. At the end of the second year, norm-referenced tests were administered; these tests were subsequently were readministered yearly in English language arts, reading, mathematics, science, and social studies. Collier and Thomas (1989) found that the group that achieved proficiency the fastest were those who entered school between ages eight and eleven. This age group reached the 50th percentile in reading within five to seven years. They also found that this group achieved the 50th percentile in mathematics in two to three years as, opposed to reading, which took five or more years. Students who arrived when they were younger than eight or older than eleven took as long as seven to ten years to achieve proficiency in English. Collier and Thomas also looked at other studies that had been done, particularly with students who continued to learn in their primary language while they were learning English. In these studies, students in bilingual programs achieved academic proficiency in English more quickly, after four to seven years. It is important to note that this study did not include students from non-literacy-oriented homes, with interrupted prior schooling experiences, or who were living in poverty. More recent research, including Hart and Risley (1995), August and Shanahan (2006, 2008), and Genesee et al. (2006), points to the importance of time as well as the type of instruction that must be provided for students, especially those with these experiences. Namely, school leaders should anticipate that students from non-literacy-oriented homes, with interrupted prior school experiences, and/or who are living in poverty will likely take much longer than high-achieving, literacy-oriented, socioeconomically advantaged students.

Does first language learning affect second language learning?

Collier and Thomas's (1989) findings, as well as those of August & Shanahan (2006) and Genesee et al. (2006), tell us a lot about second language learning, at least from the perspective of literacy-oriented students with strong first-language backgrounds. First, students who have developed grade-level or above-grade-level abilities in language arts, reading, science, social studies, and mathematics in their native language appear to learn English more quickly than do younger learners, those under the age of eight, who have not yet developed literacy skills in their primary language. Second, older ELs (over the age of 12) usually need much longer to learn English than their time in public schools may allow. Third, continuing to teach students content and language arts in their native language while they are learning English appears to be a much more effective and faster means for learning English for academic purposes for students of all ages.

However, many students do not possess school-matched, age-appropriate language skills in their strongest language. Generally, these students are non-literacy-oriented and culturally disrupted learners. They often present a dilemma for school leaders in determining whether these students should be taught in their parents' native language or English. There is much more to consider than just the language of instruction. As we will see in the chapters about content and English language learning, students from these backgrounds must receive an educational program that, besides addressing language proficiency per se, is focused on the following:

- explicit instruction that is strongly connected to students' backgrounds
- systematic and explicit development of CALP skills (i.e., the cultural, linguistic, and cognitive skills developed in literacy-oriented communities)

Many program models fail because they are not focused on these elements.

We learn language through receiving input that is meaningful, and we become literate through the same process (Krashen, 1985). By the time young children enter school, they have already had three to five years of language learning experiences. While they have the cultural, linguistic, and cognitive skills that enable them to be meaningful participants in their home communities, a good number of students do not come to school with the same package of literacy-oriented cultural, linguistic, and cognitive skills. This is an important distinction because, fundamentally, it has been found that literacy skills obtained in one language transfer to a second language (Krashen, 1985).

August and Shanahan (2006), Genesee et al. (2006), and Collier and Thomas (1989) all present findings that support this claim. In each of these studies, the group that learned the fastest had developed literacy skills in their native language. To provide effective programming, school leaders must take into account students from literacy-oriented and non-literacy-oriented backgrounds, because the two groups are on different learning trajectories, have different learning needs, and have had different life experiences.

WHAT ARE THE VARIOUS MODELS FOR ENGLISH LANGUAGE EDUCATION PROGRAMMING?

In our country, there are program models (1) that promote bilingualism and biliteracy, (2) that promote a gradual reduction of bilingualism as a means for learning English with monolingualism as its goal, and (3) in which the language of instruction is entirely in English. In most of these models, English language development, often referred to as ESL, is a component of the model. In one model, ESL classes are considered the sole means by which students learn English. How do we select the model that makes the most sense for our district? Research about which models have been found to be the most successful can help guide us in this process.

Collier and Thomas (2002) conducted a study between 1996 and 2001 in which they looked at the standardized test outcomes of over 200,000 students. The students were from the northeast, northwest, southeast, and south central regions of the United States and were enrolled in eight different program types. For the purpose of understanding the various models, the following will be provided:

- a short case example of a beginning learner of English
- a description of the program model in which the student enrolled
- Collier and Thomas's findings about the model type

Programs that promote bilingualism and biliteracy

When Ying was five years old, she moved from Beijing to Center City on the west coast of the United States. She was given some language assessments that indicated that she was a beginning-level EL. The school principal told Ying and her parents that she would have the opportunity to continue learning her native Mandarin while she learned English and that the school's goal was for her to become bilingual and biliterate in English and Mandarin. The dual language program would include an ESL class and classes in Mandarin in language arts, math, science, and social studies. The principal explained that about 90% of Ying's school day would include learning in Mandarin and the remaining 10% would be in English. He stated that this would shift to 50% in each language by the time Ying reached third grade. He also explained that fluent English speakers were enrolled in the dual language model as well. They spent 90% of their day learning in English and 10% learning in Mandarin, and the program model had the same goal of moving them to the 50/50 Mandarin/English model by third grade. Ying's parents were excited that their daughter would continue to develop her skills in Mandarin while she learned English.

Several models are based on the belief that bilingualism and biliteracy are important and preferred goals. In some of these models, ELs maintain and continue to develop their primary languages while learning English (Collier & Thomas, 2002; Soltero, 2004). These are generally referred to as *bilingual maintenance* programs. In others, such as the program that Ying enrolled in, ELs and fluent speakers of English maintain and continue to develop their primary languages while learning a second language. These are generally referred to as *bilingual immersion* programs to reflect the participation of both English-fluent and EL populations. Bilingual immersion models draw upon the belief that students learn best when they interact socially and academically in both languages and that language learning should be provided to participating students for four to six years or more. These models require a long-term commitment among parents, students, school personnel, and other stakeholders as well as a stable population of students to ensure the models' capacity to work (Howard & Christian, 2002).

In bilingual maintenance and immersion models, beginning learners of a target or second language spend most of their school day learning in their primary language and small amounts learning in the second language. As students increase their capacity to learn in the second language, classes are increased in this language. Oftentimes, these programs begin in language arts classes. These are introduced in the second language, with content classes being introduced as students develop increased skills in it. A 90/10 model is an example of this; students initially spend 90% of the school day learning in their primary language and 10% learning in the second language.

Bilingual immersion programs may begin for students in all grades. The idea behind these is that students will continue to develop in their primary language and academically while learning a target language. Bilingual immersion models are commonly introduced for children in pre-kindergarten through second grade as a 90/10 model and then gradually move to a 50/50 model. Some districts use different percentage increments for each language, and, as a result, there is wide variation among bilingual immersion programs (Goldenberg & Coleman, 2010; Soltero, 2004). Optimal bilingual immersion programs have a solid balance of ELs and fluent speakers of English. The Center for Applied Linguistics (CAL; 2009) and the Center for Research on Education, Diversity and Excellence (Howard & Christian, 2002) recommend that the total population of ELs is equal in number to the total population, or at least represents one-third to two-thirds. Ensuring that these proportions are consistent throughout the grades is critical for bilingual immersion programming.

Generally, in bilingual maintenance and immersion models, language arts is continuously taught in the primary and target languages. Table 2.2 lists the various names for these bilingual biliterate models, and Table 2.3 shows more detail on a sample model.

Table 2.2 Programs That Promote Bilingualism and Biliteracy

Program Type	Also Known As	Goal	Characteristics
Maintenance bilingual education	Developmental Enrichment Heritage language	To develop bilingualism and biliteracy	All participants are ELs.
Bilingual immersion	Dual language Two way Double immersion Two-way immersion	To develop bilingualism and biliteracy	Participants consist of both ELs and fluent English speakers.

Table 2.3 Sample of a Bilingual Biliterate Program Model

Year 1	Year 2	Year 3	Year 4
Language arts in primary language	Language arts in primary language	Language arts in primary language	Language arts in primary language
Math in primary language	Math in target language	Math in target language	Math in target language
Science in primary language	Science in primary language	Science in target language	Science in target language
Technology in primary language	Technology in primary language	Technology in primary language	Technology in primary language
Social studies in primary language	Social studies in primary language	Social studies in primary language	Social studies in primary language
Language arts in target language	Language arts in target language	Language arts in target language	Language arts in target language

Shaded cells show the transition from primary to target language.

Collier and Thomas (2002) found that students who participated in a bilingual biliterate model had the best outcome among all of the program models that they studied (see Table 2.4).

Table 2.4 English Achievement Findings From Standardized Tests of Reading for Students in Bilingual Programs

Program Type	Findings
90/10 two-way bilingual immersion: primary language is provided 90% of the time in Grades PreK–2 and gradually reduced to 50%	Students performed above grade level by Grade 5 and outperformed comparison groups.
50/50 two-way bilingual immersion	58% of students met or exceeded state standards in English reading by the end of Grades 3 and 5
50/50 one-way developmental bilingual education: one group is being educated in two languages	Students reached the 72nd percentile after four years of bilingual schooling and continued to be above grade level in Grade 7.
90/10 one-way development bilingual education: primary language is provided 90% of the time and gradually decreases to 50% by Grade 5 and continues in secondary school	Students reached the 34th percentile by end of Grade 5.

Source: Collier & Thomas, 2002.

Programs that promote the transition from the primary language to English

When Juan was five years old, he moved from Puerto Rico to a city on the east coast of the United States. His new school provided ELs with a program for gradually transitioning from Spanish to English. Juan would spend his kindergarten year receiving ESL instruction in lieu of English language arts, and his math, science, and social studies instruction would be in Spanish. Art, music, and physical education instruction would occur in English with his grade-level English-fluent classmates. In first grade, he would transition from receiving math in Spanish to receiving it in English in the general first-grade classroom. In second grade, the same transition would occur with science and social studies. In third grade, he would move fully out of the transitional bilingual education program to the general education classroom, where he would be taught solely in English.

Transitional bilingual education models like this promote a gradual reduction of the primary language as students learn English. The major goal is for students to build their capacity to learn solely in English. Typically, students begin by learning most subjects in their primary language and receiving ESL instruction. Initially, transitional programs may look like maintenance programs. However, over time, students are gradually transitioned to an all-English environment.

There are two types of transitional models (see Table 2.5). In an *early exit* program, students move from learning in the primary language to learning in English when they have demonstrated the capacity to do

Table 2.5   Programs That Promote Transitional Bilingual Education

Program Type	Goal	Characteristics
Early exit	To develop the ability to learn solely in English in general education classrooms conducted entirely in English	ELs receive instruction in their primary language and English. Students transition from learning in the primary language as their ability to learn in English increases.
Late exit	To develop the ability to learn solely in English in general education classrooms that are conducted entirely in English with a continuation of the native language for a few years after English proficiency is demonstrated	ELs receive instruction in their primary language and English. Students transition from learning in their primary language a few years after they demonstrate proficiency in English.

ordinary classroom work in English. In a *late exit* program, students continue to learn in the primary language for a few more years after they have demonstrated proficiency in English. Most programs in the United States are early-exit programs (Soltero, 2004) and do not yield the same successes as do late-exit programming. Table 2.6 shows more detail on a sample transitional program.

Table 2.6 Sample of a Transitional Bilingual Education Model

Year 1	Year 2	Year 3	Year 4
Language arts in primary language	Language arts in primary language	Language arts in primary language	Language arts taught in general English-instructed classroom
Math in primary language	Math taught in general English-instructed classroom	Math taught in general English-instructed classroom	Math taught in general English-instructed classroom
Science/ technology in primary language	Science/ technology in primary language	Science/ technology taught in general English-instructed classroom	Science/ technology taught in general English-instructed classroom
Social studies in primary language	Social studies in primary language	Social studies in primary language	Social studies taught in general English-instructed classroom
English as a second language	English as a second language	English as a second language	English language arts taught in general English-instructed classroom

Shaded cells show the transition from primary to target language.

Collier and Thomas's (2002) study also included outcomes of students who participated in transitional bilingual educational programming. Table 2.7 describes their finding that students who participated in late-exit programs had better outcomes than students in early-exit programs.

Table 2.7   English Achievement Findings From Standardized Tests of Reading for Students in Transitional Bilingual Education Models

Program Type	Findings
90/10 transitional bilingual education: 90% of Grades PreK–2 instruction is in primary language, and this decreases until Grade 5 when all instruction is in English in the general education classroom	Students reached the 32nd percentile by end of Grade 5.
50/50 transitional bilingual education: instruction is 50% in both primary and target languages for three to four years, followed with English immersion in the general education classroom	Students achieved the 47th percentile by Grade 11.

Source: Collier & Thomas, 2002.

Programs that use English to teach English

Example 1

When Lily was five years old, she moved from Poland to a small town in the Midwestern United States. She had never been exposed to English, and language testing found her to be a beginning learner. In her new school, she left her kindergarten classroom to meet with her ESL teacher, who gave her instruction for 90 minutes a day. The rest of the day, Lily remained with her English-fluent classmates in the classroom. Her kindergarten teacher had never worked with an EL and received no specialized help to do so.

Example 2

When Fernanda moved from Cape Verde to Massachusetts at the age of five, she had never been taught in English. She was placed in a kindergarten classroom with a teacher who had been trained to teach English and content to ELs. Twice a week, Fernanda left class for 30 minutes to work with an ESL teacher.

Example 3

When Vladimir moved from Ukraine to New York at the age of five, he too had never been exposed to English. He was placed in a kindergarten classroom with a teacher who had been trained to teach ELs. He also was provided with a bilingual Russian/English-speaking aide who helped him understand his classes and become acquainted with his new school and classmates. Every day for an hour, Vladimir's ESL teacher came into his class and provided him and the other ELs with instruction in English.

Generally, programs that use only English with ELs include ESL classes. They can also, but do not always, include content classes that are specifically designed and delivered for students to learn English as they learn content. This is commonly called *sheltered English immersion* and/or *content-based ESL* (Echevarria, Vogt, & Short, 2000; Soltero, 2004). Further, these programs can, but do not always, include bilingual support or clarification in the native language, whereby instruction is delivered in English and explained in the primary language as needed. This model is often used when there are speakers of many different languages and not enough of any one language to implement bilingual programming. Table 2.8 lists the various names for this model, and Tables 2.9 and 2.10 show more detail on sample models.

Table 2.8   Programs That Are Taught Only in English

Program Type	Also known as	Goal	Characteristics
Structured English immersion	Pull out Push in Content-based ESL ESL pull out ESL	To develop the ability to learn solely in English in general education classrooms conducted entirely in English	Model taught entirely in English with little to no support in the native language

Table 2.9   Sample of a Structured English Immersion Model That Includes Content Classes

Year 1	Year 2	Year 3	Year 4
English as a second language	English as a second language	English as a second language	English language arts in general classroom
Math taught using structured format	Math taught using structured format	Math taught in general classroom	Math taught in general classroom
Science/technology taught using structured format	Science/technology taught using structured format	Science/technology taught in general classroom	Science/technology taught in general classroom
Social studies taught using structured format	Social studies taught using structured format	Social studies taught using structured format	Social studies taught in general classroom

Shaded cells show the transition from primary to target language.

Table 2.10 Sample of a Structured English Immersion/ESL Pull-Out Model

Year 1	Year 2	Year 3	Year 4
English as a second language	English as a second language	English as a second language	English taught in general class
Math taught in English in general classroom	Math taught in English in general classroom	Math taught in English in general classroom	Math taught in English in general classroom
Science/technology taught in English in general classroom	Science/technology taught in English in general classroom	Science/technology taught in English in general classroom	Science/technology taught in English in general classroom
Social studies taught in English in general classroom	Social studies taught in English in general classroom	Social studies taught in English in general classroom	Social studies taught in English in general classroom

Shaded cells show the transition from primary to target language.

In Table 2.11, you can see the results of Collier and Thomas's (2002) study regarding ELs who participated in program models that used English to teach English. Generally, students did not fare well in this model.

Table 2.11 English Achievement Findings From Standardized Tests of Reading for Students in Programs Using English to Teach English

Program Type	Findings
ESL content classes provided for two to three years, followed by immersion in general education classes	Average score on tests were at the 23rd percentile by high school.

Source: Collier & Thomas, 2002.

Researchers from the Center for Applied Linguistics and the Center for Research on Education, Diversity and Excellence worked closely with teachers to secure a better-articulated model of sheltering instruction. Through years of research and collaboration with teachers, they developed the Sheltered Instruction Observation Protocol (SIOP; Echevarria, Vogt, & Short, 2000). The model includes eight elements for planning and delivering instruction and providing clarification in the native language. While the SIOP model is not intended for beginning learners of English, when it has been employed by teachers who are trained in using it, student performance has been found to increase dramatically. The researchers claim that the model works well with students from a variety of prior schooling experiences and in a variety of classroom situations, including those solely composed of ELs as well as those with ELs and fluent speakers of English. Because of this work, it may be that the conclusions we draw about the efficacy of various program models from Collier and Thomas's (2002) study need to be refined.

What happens when students are provided with no support to learn English?

When Alberto moved to New York from Colombia, his parents refused to let him participate in the bilingual program in his new school. They believed that he would be better off in the general kindergarten classroom with his English-fluent peers.

As Figure 2.12 shows, Collier and Thomas's (2002) study also looked at the educational outcomes of students like Alberto, whose parents refused to have their children participate in any programming for ELs. Sadly, this group did the poorest among all of the groups.

Table 2.12   Findings for Students With No Specialized Language Programming

Program Type	Findings
No specialized language programming for ELs	Students performed significantly less well in math by Grade 5 than peers in bilingual programs and had highest dropout rate among all groups. Those remaining in school scored at the 25th percentile on standardized reading tests during their high school years.

Source: Collier & Thomas, 2002.

Program models that are targeted for students with limited prior schooling

As mentioned earlier in this chapter, it is quite common for ELs to come from non-literacy-oriented communities or have culturally disrupted circumstances. It is essential that these students' learning needs be intentionally addressed as they learn English. In addition, children from non-literacy-oriented communities who are recent immigrants may have limited or no prior schooling. Perhaps schooling is just not central to that community in their home country, or perhaps they experienced disruptions in their home country, such as war, civil disturbance, or severe economic deprivation. Students like this do not have proficiency in their primary language or English; have large gaps in their education; have limited or no literacy skills; are often many years behind their peers in terms of grade-level knowledge; and lack the necessary basic skills, content knowledge, and critical thinking (CALP) skills. These circumstances obviously provide schools with challenges.

To meet these challenges, many schools have implemented programming specifically designed for ELs with limited or no prior schooling. In addition, several resources are available to support educators in meeting the needs of this population (Calderón, 2007; Calderón & Minaya-Rowe, 2010; Pransky, 2008). Table 2.13 describes this type of programming, and Table 2.14 shows more detail on a sample model. The following characteristics are commonly found in programs that are targeted for students from these backgrounds (Echevarria, Short, & Powers, 2005; Freeman & Freeman, 2002; Short & Boyson, 2003; Soltero, 2004):

- is separate from what is offered to the general student population
- specifically addresses the particular gaps and learning needs of student
- includes courses in English language, literacy development, and American cultural practices
- uses curriculum materials targeted to students' English proficiency levels
- adapts instruction often using theme-based units of study
- allocates the appropriate amount of personnel resources needed to address students' needs
- contains an outreach component to families to build connections between the school, family, and student
- is taught in English or the primary language of students

Table 2.13   Programs for Students With Limited Prior Schooling

Program Type	Also Known As	Goal	Characteristics
Programs for students with limited prior schooling	Newcomer programs	To learn English and catch up with peers in order to be able to handle grade-level content	Instruction may be in the primary language or English, and the population typically includes secondary-aged students. Programming is separate from the general education classroom. Personnel resources are allocated to provide instruction in English and content.

Table 2.14   Sample of Programs for Students With Limited Prior Schooling

Year 1	Year 2	Year 3
English as a second language	English as a second language	English as a second language
Math taught at student's academic level*	Math taught at student's academic level*	Math taught at student's academic level*
Science/technology taught at student's academic level*	Science/technology taught at student's academic level*	Science/technology taught at student's academic level*
Social studies taught at student's academic level*	Social studies taught at student's academic level*	Social studies taught at student's academic level*

*May be taught in English, the primary language, and/or English with clarification support in the primary language.

What does the research tell us?

Whether students are enrolled in bilingual maintenance or sheltered English models, these models are more effective when they incorporate the native language (Francis, Lesaux, & August, 2006; Goldenberg & Coleman, 2010; Slavin & Cheung, 2005). At the same time, selecting a program model is dependent on a number of variables. Many believe that there is no one program model that is the best for all students (August & Hakuta, 1997; Genesee, 1999). Rather, it is important to consider the following when designing a program for ELs:

- its context within a specific school and/or district
- the needs of the students and the resources available for implementation
- the number of students involved
- the languages and grades that students represent
- whether students are from literacy-oriented, non-literacy-oriented, or culturally disrupted communities
- students' prior school experiences

Regardless of which program is chosen, there can be no doubt that the quality and overall effectiveness of programming depends on the structures that leaders create to support implementation. In the next chapter, we will discuss the steps for selecting the program model(s) for your school.

REFERENCES

American Institutes for Research & WestEd. (2002). *Effects of the implementation of Proposition 227 on the education of English learners, K–12: Year 2 report.* Retrieved December 10, 2010, from http://www.wested.org/online_pubs/year2finalrpt .pdf

August, D., & Hakuta, K. (1997). *Improving schooling for language-minority children: A research agenda.* Washington, DC: National Academy Press.

August, D., & Shanahan, T. (2006). *Literacy in second language learners: Report of the National Literacy Panel on Language Minority Children and Youth.* Mahwah, NJ: Lawrence Erlbaum.

August, D., & Shanahan, T. (2008). *Developing reading and writing in second language learners: Lessons from a report of the National Literacy Panel on Language Minority Children and Youth.* New York: Routledge.

Baker, C. (2006). Foundations of bilingual education and bilingualism (4th ed.). Tonawanda, NY: Multilingual Matters.

Burdick-Will, J., & Gomez, C. (2006). *Assimilation versus multiculturalism: Bilingual education and the Latino challenge.* Mahwah, NJ: Lawrence Erlbaum.

Calderón, M. (2007). *Teaching reading to English language learners 6–12: A framework for improving achievement in content areas.* Thousand Oaks, CA: Corwin.

Calderón, M. E., & Minaya-Rowe, L. (2010). *Preventing long-term ELs: Transforming schools to meet core standards.* Thousand Oaks, CA: Corwin.

Center for Applied Linguistics. (2009). *What is two-way immersion?* Retrieved December 10, 2010, from http://www.cal.org/twi/FAQ/faq1.htm

Collier, V., & Thomas, W. (1989). How quickly can immigrants become proficient in school English? *Journal of Educational Issues of Language Minority Students, 5,* 26–38.

Collier, V., & Thomas, W. (2002). A national study of school effectiveness for language minority students' long-term academic achievement. Santa Cruz, CA: Center for Research on Education, Diversity and Excellence. Retrieved December 10, 2010, from http://eric.ed.gov/ERICWebPortal/contentdelivery/ servlet/ERICServlet?accno=ED436087

Crawford, J. (1996). *Bilingual education: History, politics, theory and practice.* Los Angeles: Bilingual Education Services.

Cummins, J. (1981). Age on arrival and immigrant second language learning in Canada: A reassessment. *Applied Linguistics, 2,* 132–149.

Cummins, J. (2000). Language, power, and pedagogy: Bilingual children in the crossfire. Clevedon, UK: Multilingual Matters.

Cummins, J., & Swain, M. (1986). *Bilingualism in education.* New York: Longman.

Dunklee, D. R., & Shoop, R. J. (2006). *The principal's quick guide to school law: Reducing liability, litigation and other potential legal tangles.* Thousand Oaks, CA: Corwin.

Echevarria, J., Short, D., & Powers, K. (2005). School reform and standards-based education: How do teachers help English language learners? Retrieved December 13, 2010, from http://wikiedresearch.wdfiles.com/local—files/ bilingual-education/SIOP.pdf

Echevarria, J., Vogt, M. E., & Short, D. J. (2000). *Making English comprehensible: The SIOP model.* New York: Pearson.

Freeman, Y. S., & Freeman, D. E. (with Mercuri, S.). (2002). *Closing the achievement gap: How to reach limited-formal schooling and long-term English learners.* Portsmouth, NH: Heinemann.

Francis, D., Lesaux, M., & August, D. (2006). Language of instruction. In D. August & T. Shanahan (Eds.), *Developing literacy in second-language learners: Report of the National Literacy Panel on Language-Minority Children and Youth* (pp. 365–413). Mahwah, NJ: Lawrence Erlbaum.

Genesee, F. (Ed.). (1999). *Program alternatives for linguistically diverse students.* Santa Cruz, CA: Center for Research on Education, Diversity and Excellence.

Genesee, F., Lindholm-Leary, K., Saunders, W., & Christian, D. (2006). *Educating English language learners.* New York: Cambridge University Press.

Goldenberg, C., & Coleman, R. (2010). *Promoting academic achievement among English learners: A guide to the research.* Thousand Oaks: Corwin.

Gonzalez, R. D. (2000). Critical perspectives of the English Only movement (Vol. 1). Mahwah, NJ: Lawrence Erlbaum.

Hart, B., & Risley, T. R. (1995). *Meaningful differences in everyday experiences of young American children.* Baltimore: Paul H. Brookes.

Horn, C. L., & Kurlaender, M. (2006). *The end of Keyes: Resegregation trends and achievement in Denver Public Schools.* Cambridge, MA: The Civil Rights Project at Harvard University.

Howard, E. R., & Christian, D. (2002). *Two-way immersion 101: Designing and implementing a two-way immersion program at the elementary level.* Santa Cruz, CA: Center for Research on Education, Diversity and Excellence. Retrieved December 10, 2010, from http://www.cal.org/crede/pdfs/epr9.pdf

Krashen, S. (1985). *The input hypothesis: Issues and implications.* Beverly Hills, CA: Laredo Publishing Company.

Mendoza, M., & Ayala, H. (1999). *English language education for children in public schools.* Retrieved December 10, 2010, from http://www.onenation.org/aztext.html

Mid-Atlantic Equity Consortium. (1995). *Legal responsibilities of education agencies serving language minority students.* Retrieved December 13, 2010, from http://www.maec.org/legal.html

Montero, R., & Chavez, J. (2001). *Be it enacted by the people of the State of Colorado.* Retrieved December 10, 2010, from http://www.onenation.org/cotext.html

National Association of Bilingual Education. (2009). *What is bilingual education?* Retrieved December 10, 2010, from http://www.nabe.org/bilingualed.html

Osorio-O'Dea, P. (2001). *Bilingual education: An overview.* Retrieved December 10, 2010, from http://www.policyalmanac.org/education/archive/bilingual.pdf

Pransky, K. (2008). *Beneath the surface: The hidden realities of teaching culturally and linguistically diverse young learners, K–6.* Portsmouth, NH: Heinemann.

Reese, J. (2005). *America's public schools: From the common school to "No Child Left Behind."* Baltimore: Johns Hopkins University Press.

Short, D. J., & Boyson, B. A. (2003). *Establishing an effective newcomer program.* Washington, DC: Center for Applied Linguistics. Retrieved December 10, 2010, from http://www.cal.org/resources/Digest/digest_pdfs/0312short.pdf

Slavin, R., & Cheung, A. (2005). A synthesis of research on language of reading instruction for English language learners. *Review of Educational Research, 75,* 247–281.

Soltero, S. W. (2004). *Dual language: Teaching and learning in two languages.* New York: Pearson.

Tamayo, L., Porter, R., & Rossell, C. (2001). *An initiative petition for a law: An act relative to the teaching of English in public schools.* Retrieved December 20, 2009, from http://www.onenation.org/matext.html

Teachers of English to Speakers of Other Languages. (2006). *PreK–12 English language proficiency standards.* Alexandria, VA: Author.

Unz, R., & Tuchman, G. M. (1997). *English language education for children in public schools.* Retrieved December 10, 2010, from http://www.onenation.org/fulltext.html

Uriarte, M., & Karp, F. (2009). *English language learners in Massachusetts: Trends in enrollments and outcomes.* Boston: Mauricio Gaston Institute for Latino Development and Public Policy. Retrieved December 10, 2010, from http://www.gaston.umb.edu/UserFiles/09ELLsinMA%20brief.pdf

U.S. Department of Education. (2002). No Child Left Behind: A desktop reference. Retrieved December 10, 2010, from http://www2.ed.gov/admins/lead/account/nclbreference/reference.pdf

U.S. Department of Education, Office of Civil Rights. (2000). *The provision of an equal education opportunity to limited-English proficient students.* Retrieved December 10, 2010, from http://www.ed.gov/about/offices/list/ocr/eeolep/index.html

U.S. Department of Education, Office of Civil Rights. (2005). *Programs for English language learners: Part IV: Glossary.* Retrieved December 10, 2010, from http://www.ed.gov/about/offices/list/ocr/ell/edlite-glossary.html

U.S. Department of Justice, Office of Civil Rights. (2003). *Title VI of the Civil Rights Act of 1964.* Retrieved December 10, 2010, from http://www.justice.gov/crt/cor/coord/titlevi.php

3

Selecting Effective Program Models

W hen Mr. Paxton, an elementary school principal, began working at Main Street School in a small city, he learned that a significant number of non-English-speaking families had moved into a newly opened apartment complex and that their children would be attending his school. Assuming that the children would be English learners (ELs), he began to consider the various English language education program model options that would work best for the students and his school. What steps should Mr. Paxton take as he makes this important decision?

In this chapter we will discuss the various steps that should be involved in selecting appropriate program models.

IDENTIFYING ELs

Initially, the most important step involves identifying and sorting the ELs in each school. This information is needed to determine the program model or models that are best suited. The following questions are intended to help in the sorting process:

1. What steps are needed for effectively identifying ELs?

2. What additional information should be included about the students to select, plan, and deliver the most effective model?

A *home language survey* is by far the most common means and tool to determine who might or might not be an EL (see Resource 3.1 for a sample). It is intended as a means for determining who should be assessed. The purpose is not to decide who is and is not an EL. This document should be furnished to parents at enrollment, one for each enrollee, as a means for initially sorting the students who use a language other than English. For example, Mr. Paxton will include this as part of the enrollment forms that parents will complete.

One might think that, because the dominant population in most of the nation's schools is monolingual speakers of English, a home language survey seems like a nice but unnecessary, or even impractical idea. A school may decide that it can figure out on its own which families should be given the survey. But how would a school know? Would it be when a parent speaks with an accent? This may lead to unintended discriminatory practices, and a school may miss many potential ELs if done by guesswork alone. Therefore, a home language survey should be given to each and every new enrollee. The sample survey provided in Resource 3.1 includes a series of questions about a child's language use with family members and others as well as a few questions about prior schooling.

If the answer to any question on the home language survey indicates that a child uses a language other than English (e.g., if the child uses another language when speaking with friends or a grandparent), the child must be assessed to determine whether he or she is an EL. As we learned in Chapter 2, it is a federal regulation that potential ELs be identified. The home language survey is a crucial first step in this process.

However, this survey should not be the only means for identifying language-minority students. Some parents may indicate that their children use only English when that is, in fact, not the case. This may occur for a variety of reasons, including the fear that their children will not be allowed to attend school or will not be treated like other children. When a school suspects that a student may be an EL, the student must be assessed.

Identification Testing

Testing must include, where age-appropriate, assessing a student's ability to listen, speak, read, and write in English. It is not uncommon for a student to test proficient in listening and speaking but not in reading and writing. The federal definition of an EL is a student who is not yet able to do ordinary class work in English. The capacity to do ordinary work requires English proficiency in all four areas: listening, speaking, reading, and writing. The purpose of the assessments is threefold:

- identifying a student's need for EL services
- establishing an EL's English proficiency level
- determining the number of ELs in a district and their English language and learning needs

There are a number of reliable commercially available screening tests that are specifically designed for identifying ELs. In alphabetical order, the following are five commonly used English language proficiency tests:

- Bilingual Syntax Measure (BSM) of listening and speaking
- IDEA Proficiency Test (IPT)
- Language Assessment Scales (LAS)
- WIDA-ACCESS Placement Test
- Woodcock-Muñoz Language Survey–Revised (WMLS-R)

Resource 3.2 includes information for ordering these assessments. Some districts use the listening and speaking components of one test in combination with the reading and writing components of another. For example, they use the BSM to test listening and speaking and the LAS to test reading and writing. With the exception of the WIDA test, English and Spanish versions of these tests are available.

Assessment in the primary language

It is very helpful, when possible, to test students in both their primary language and English, and this is essential for planning and implementing bilingual programming. It provides key information about a student's ability to listen, speak, read, and write in both languages. For example, students from literacy-oriented backgrounds may perform at the proficient level in Spanish and the pre-production level in English, whereas students from non-literacy-oriented experiences may perform at a lower proficiency level in Spanish.

The Student Oral Language Observation Matrix (SOLOM) was developed by the California Department of Education to assess students' ability to listen and speak in any language (Lindholm-Leary, 2001). It is particularly helpful for assessing the primary languages of students who speak languages other than English and Spanish. To administer the SOLOM, an assessor observes a student engaging in listening and speaking tasks and then rates the student's skills in these tasks according to five language areas: comprehension, fluency, vocabulary, pronunciation, and grammar (see Resource 3.3 for a sample of the SOLOM). The assessor must be fully proficient in the language being assessed. As with any identification testing, an assessment of reading and writing should also accompany the SOLOM results.

Administrators may wish to have their own identification assessments created in English and/or another language by knowledgeable staff. They should check with their state department of education to ensure that the identification testing that is used is in compliance with state requirements.

When should identification testing be done?

Potential ELs should be tested as soon as possible. State regulations may require schools to complete identification testing within a certain period of time after enrollment. A good rule of thumb is to assess a student within his or her first five days at school. There are two very good reasons for completing identification testing quickly:

1. It allows a school to determine programming needs as soon as possible.
2. It enables students who have been identified as ELs to receive appropriate programming as soon as possible.

Allocating staff and time for testing

School leaders should consult with their state department of education to determine whether those who identify ELs are properly licensed to do so. Generally, ESL and bilingual education teachers are trained to administer identification testing and should be the ones to do it. In the absence of this, school administrators must make every effort to assign and train staff to do this task according to their state regulations. They must also ensure that there is enough staff for all of the testing that needs to be done. Further, whoever is assigned to do it must be proficient in the language that is being tested.

Most testing is administered individually and may take anywhere from just a couple of minutes (e.g., if a child is completely non-English-speaking) to an hour or more; the more language proficiency a student has, and the older the student, the longer the assessment period will probably take. The time needed to complete this task is important to factor into one's planning. It is helpful for districts to keep a record of the time that it takes to conduct their identification testing and to use these calculations from year to year to estimate the time needed for it. School leaders, especially those in districts with large numbers of ELs, should also calculate the anticipated number of enrollees per year and the hours needed for testing so that this activity can be completed successfully in the shortest time possible. It is also important that the testing be done in a comfortable, quiet location to ensure the most accurate results. This may mean having staff travel to the school in which the student is enrolled or training staff in each school to provide the testing. Districts that have central registration centers should allocate appropriate space for identification testing to occur.

Documenting language proficiency test findings

Documenting test findings is important. Resource 3.4 provides a sample document for summarizing test findings, as well as tracking student growth. This and the home language survey provide key information about the ELs who have been identified.

Including a parent and/or
student interview when an EL is identified

As essential as they are, neither the home language survey nor EL testing provide information about a student's prior schooling and other relevant background information. When a student is identified as an EL, it is important for school leaders to gather such information. This is particularly true for students with interrupted formal education and students from non-literacy-oriented backgrounds. An interview with the parents and/or their child is an important next step. Resource 3.5 is intended to support districts in this activity. Parents and students should be provided with bilingual translators, as needed, to conduct the interview or provide the needed interpreting support for the interview.

Analyzing home language survey,
testing, and interview findings

The initial analysis of home language survey, EL assessment, and interview data guides school leaders in selecting the most appropriate EL program model(s) for their school or district. Programming should be understood as an inclusive way for a school's ELs to be active learners in and members of their school community. The more information that is gathered, the better the chances are that the program model will be successful.

Determining commonalities and differences in the data is crucial for selecting the most appropriate program model. For example: Do many of the district's ELs speak the same primary language? Are they in the same grades, separated among all of the grades, or scattered throughout the district? Are there commonalities in their English proficiency levels? Resource 3.6 was created to help districts sort and collate the findings of the assessment/enrollment process and select program models. Each category has been separated by grade as well as by the following:

- first language
- country of origin
- English proficiency level
- interrupted or limited prior schooling
- receiving free or reduced lunch
- receiving Title 1 services

Program model options will become clearer through the analysis process. For example, a district may find that it has many speakers of the same language and that a bilingual program model is, therefore, an appropriate choice.

Selecting a work group to develop or revise program model(s)

Case example: By analyzing data about actual students, Mr. Paxton learned that there would be 34 ELs enrolling in his school, 23 of whom spoke Mandarin. Some of their families had moved to the city to work in local Chinese restaurants and others to work in one of the city's agricultural companies. Through the parent interviews that were conducted, Mr. Paxton learned that some of the ELs were from literacy-oriented backgrounds and others from non-literacy-oriented backgrounds. In addition, there were two Egyptian speakers of Arabic, five Puerto Rican speakers of Spanish, and four Brazilian speakers of Portuguese. A few of these students were also from non-literacy-oriented backgrounds and, because of their families' socioeconomic status, would be participating in the school's free lunch program.

Mr. Paxton invited parent and community representatives from each of the language groups to join a work group that would advise his selection of a program model for the children. Bilingual translators were also included to ensure that parents and school personnel could communicate well and that parents would feel welcome and comfortable. Initially, some of the parents did not want their children to participate in any specialized program. They assumed that their children would learn English more quickly if they remained in the general English-instructed classroom. The work group meetings provided time for the parents to learn about the value of EL programs, and various research-based models for those programs, while school personnel learned much about the families and their communities. This laid the foundation for a very important relationship built on mutual respect and trust between the school and the families, which had many long-term benefits aside from the specific task of discussing program models.

The work group recommended a *late-exit model* of transitional bilingual education for its Mandarin speakers, and a *structured English immersion model* with clarification in the native language for the other language groups. Parental participation in this process also helped the school secure the bilingual staff and native language tutors that would be needed.

Like Mr. Paxton chose to do, the U.S. Department of Education (2005) suggests that districts organize working groups for developing EL programming and that they include the following groups:

- school leaders and teachers, including teachers of ELs and general classroom teachers
- parents
- students
- community representatives who work with ELs

A comprehensive plan is more likely to occur with support from these stakeholders. The case example highlights the importance of work groups in selecting a program model or more than one model.

Gathering descriptions and information about various program model options that are based on sound research

Whether a district is new to providing programming for its ELs or expanding and/or revising its programming, it is important that it select a research-based model that is the most likely to be successful for ensuring that ELs achieve the following goals:

- become proficient in English
- learn subject matter at grade level
- are integrated with English-fluent peers and members of the school community

Resource 3.7 provides suggested readings about particular program models. These can greatly assist work groups in selecting and implementing program models.

In addition, the goals for ELs should be the same as for non-EL students; that is, the goals for all students should be inclusive of ELs.

Defining the goals of the work group

The following questions are intended to support the work group:

1. How will the selected model promote the overall goals and vision of the district?

2. How will it address the English language development and content learning needs of all of the ELs who have been identified?

3. What staffing and resources are needed to support this EL program model?

4. How will the model support, as seamlessly as possible, a transition to the general English-instructed program?

5. What methods will be used to determine the effectiveness of the model and any changes that are needed to strengthen its outcome?

It is fundamental that the program model provide ELs with meaningful access to the school district's educational programming. Each district has its own particular, individual circumstances as well as mission and vision for its students, and the program that is selected for its ELs should strongly relate to these. Figure 3.1 helps guide us in the program selection process.

Figure 3.1   Selection Process Using a Whole-School Context

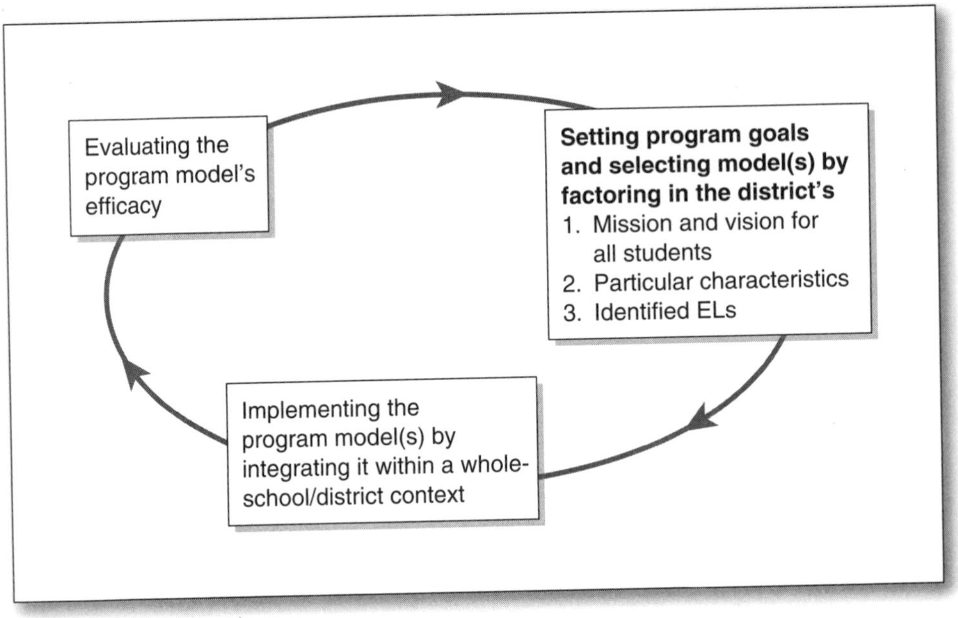

Evaluating the program model's efficacy

Setting program goals and selecting model(s) by factoring in the district's
1. Mission and vision for all students
2. Particular characteristics
3. Identified ELs

Implementing the program model(s) by integrating it within a whole-school/district context

Selecting program model(s)

School leaders must also determine the time frame in which the goals for its particular ELs will be reached and how success will be measured. In Chapter 2, we learned that there are ELs from literacy and non-literacy, culturally disrupted, and/or limited-prior-schooling backgrounds. While the goal for all ELs is to be able to perform ordinary class work in English independently, this is not a monolithic group. Ensuring that this goal is attained involves thinking about the needs of specific groups of learners. A school needs to create and implement a differentiated program model while integrating it within the context of the whole school. To do this, school leaders must take into account the school's mission and vision for all learners.

One mistake to avoid is creating one set of program characteristics and expectations for all ELs. Doing so usually disadvantages non-literacy-oriented and culturally disrupted learners, the very students who need the most attention. In the case presented earlier, for example, Mr. Paxton learned that some of the students in his school were from non-literacy-oriented homes and lived in poverty. He ensured that they were provided with additional supports and time to learn English and subject matter. He also created a study group in which his teachers read a book about students from these backgrounds (see Resource 3.7 for resource suggestions on this topic). Another mistake to avoid, one that is often made unintentionally, is segregating ELs. This may occur because programming is thought of as separate from, and not part of, a whole-school community. Indeed, whether it is done unintentionally or intentionally, segregation of linguistic-minority students is known to be a problem in U.S. schools (Gándara, 2010) and should be avoided. ELs can be in isolated schools and isolated within one school. In both cases, it may not yield positive results in terms of ELs' academic performance and membership or status in their school community (Cohen & Lotan, 1995; Constantino de Cohen & Clewell, 2007). Mr. Paxton wisely considered the ways in which the ELs in his school would be actively engaged in learning communities with English-fluent peers.

Reexamining a school or district mission, vision, and distinct characteristics

An important step in selecting a program model is to reexamine the core mission and vision in order to figure out optimal ways in which the EL program will complement and expand them. For example, a school district may have found that its core mission is to value diversity. While this mission may have been formed to honor students with learning differences and disabilities, the implementation of a program model for ELs can fit quite nicely with this mission. The same district may be located in a rural farming community and thus designed and implemented its curriculum to connect with its environment. ELs and their families may not be familiar with this farming context and will need the opportunity to learn about it in a meaningful way. Similarly, a school within a district may be designated as the site for students with significant disabilities. If it is decided that the program model for ELs is to be implemented in this school, efforts should be made to help the two programs be part of the school community as a whole and not two separate programs within the school.

Integrating a program model within a whole-school context

As the various program models are examined, school leaders must take time to determine how the model will be integrated meaningfully within the school. This requires a real examination of and reflection about the everyday routines that occur and how these will interact seamlessly with the program model that is implemented. It also requires school leaders to become familiar with ELs and their families and take additional steps to reexamine various common school activities to ensure that they are understood meaningfully by the EL community.

Case example 1: Mrs. Fields sent her students home with a permission slip for a field trip to the science museum. When Tren, a Vietnamese EL, heard the phrase *going on a field trip,* he was afraid that the school would be taking him away from his family. Acting on his fears, he did not bring the note home to his parents. Because he did not have a permission slip, he had to be left behind—the only one of his classmates not to go on the trip.

Case example 2: During Mr. Paxton's second year as the principal of Main Street School, a religious group sponsored a number of Somali refugees to live in the community. When they enrolled the Somali children in his school, he conducted a parent interview, with the help of a translator, and learned that the children had not had any prior formal schooling, dressed very differently than their American peers, and had different dietary customs. To help the families feel welcome and learn more about the community, Mr. Paxton decided to meet with them during the first month of school. To prepare for the meeting, he also made plans to meet with community representatives who were familiar with the Somali families.

In addition to the findings that are gathered about the identified ELs, the following items should be considered to better ensure that effective programming is implemented. School leaders should plan these with the work group, teachers of ELs, and other stakeholders to ensure that they are as successful as possible:

- the district's or school's familiarity, experience, and preparation to work with the specific ELs who have been identified
- the ways in which ELs and their families will be meaningfully informed about the school's routine practices and activities
- the professional development needs of the district to teach its ELs
- curriculum development for teaching ESL and content to its ELs
- parent involvement

Regardless of the program model that is selected, it is important for school leaders, teachers, and others who work with ELs to learn as much as possible about the students and their families. Routine practices such as open houses, field trips, parent conferences, and post–high school planning, including the college application process, are often taken for granted as known activities when, in reality, they are not familiar to many ELs and their families (Zacarian, 2007).

As we will discuss in Chapter 6, teachers and school leaders must undertake a fact-finding mission to learn as much as possible about their EL community in order to implement tasks and activities that complement its various linguistic and cultural representatives (Bailey & Pransky, 2005; Delpit, 2006; Faltis, 2005; Pransky, 2008).

The role of a student's primary language

The primary languages of students should be a critical component of any program. When there are critical masses of ELs who represent the same primary language and who are in the same grade, a bilingual biliteracy model of bilingual immersion (e.g., dual language) has been shown to be highly effective for promoting language learning and value (Cummins, 2002; Soltero, 2004). When implementing a bilingual immersion program, it is best to begin at an early grade, such as kindergarten, and to build programming by adding another grade level each successive year. The intent must be that English-fluent students and ELs will become bilingual biliterate and that both languages will be used for instruction from elementary grades through high school graduation.

An alternative good choice, when there aren't representatives of a primary language other than English in the grade levels associated with a bilingual immersion model, is a *maintenance bilingual education* or late-exit *transitional bilingual education* program because of the merits that have been found in maintaining a student's primary language while they are learning English. As we will examine in this book, each transition from one level of English proficiency to the next is a significant one for ELs in transitional models because it means that less language support will be provided. Late-exit transitional bilingual education programs give students much-needed time to fine-tune their understanding of English while becoming active members of their school community.

Many schools, however, do not have the population of ELs needed for these bilingual program models. In these cases, a sheltered immersion model with clarification support in the native language may be a good solution. This support may be provided by teachers, aides, and/or volunteers. No matter what model is used, whenever possible, the primary languages of students should be included.

Bilingual programming indicators

A critical mass of students who speak the same language is needed for bilingual maintenance, immersion, and transitional bilingual education models. In some states, it is required that bilingual education be provided when a specific number of students speak the same language. Districts should consult with their state department of education to ascertain this important information. For example, bilingual education programming is required in New York when there are more than 20 identified ELs whose primary language is the same and who are in the same grade and school (New York State Department of Education, 2010). When it is determined that bilingual education programming is either required or desired, schools must decide which type of bilingual education programming will serve them best.

Bilingual immersion models

An immersion model may be an ideal choice in districts that value bilingualism. It provides a solid means for ELs and English-fluent students to develop bilingual skills, learn academic content successfully, and engage in positive social and academic cross-cultural and language experiences. As we learned in Chapter 2, this type of programming is optimally provided when there is a balance of students representing both language groups, and one third to one half of the total should be ELs. Further, a long-term plan that begins in kindergarten and includes a minimum of four to six years is required. In addition, school administrators must decide how much students will engage in the study of each language at the various grade levels. This decision is quite dependent on the following:

1. The number of trained and appropriately licensed or prepared personnel to deliver instruction in English and the second language chosen

2. Curriculum materials that are available in both languages

3. Transition plans for secondary schooling

4. Parent, community, and schoolwide support, including parents of ELs and English-fluent speakers

5. School leaders' capacity to advocate for the program among staff, parents, and the community and to integrate it within the school

6. Long-term commitment of at least four to six years for the model to be effective

Bringing work groups composed of English-fluent and EL parents together is critical in the formation and sustained continuation of a bilingual immersion program. Unlike other program models, it requires the continuous commitment among the two language populations for its existence. It simply cannot exist without a balanced student population and committed teachers and parents. Resource 3.7 provides bilingual immersion work groups and others with suggested reading about the theoretical underpinnings and practical applications of the model.

Staffing considerations

There must be resources for implementing any program model. For example, a bilingual immersion model requires teachers who are fluent in both languages at each of the grade levels involved. In Chapter 1, we learned that many of the nation's teachers are not trained to work with ELs and that administrators must take steps to ensure that they receive this training. An important component of the training is that staff know and understand the model that has been chosen and its purpose. This will help them in making instructional decisions that are more intentionally targeted for the model's success. Districts should consult with local colleges and universities, their state department of education, and educational service agencies to create a professional development plan that is targeted for building and sustaining a trained workforce in the chosen program

RESOURCE 3.2
Commonly Used Identification Tests
(in alphabetical order)

Bilingual Syntax Measure (BSM)

The Bilingual Syntax Measure is an individually administered assessment of listening and speaking produced by Pearson. It is intended for preschool through Grade 12 and is available in English and Spanish. Information about it may be found online at www.pearsonassessments.com/HAIWEB/Cultures/en-us/Productdetail.htm?Pid=015-8015-983&Mode=summary.

IDEA Proficiency Test (IPT)

The IDEA Proficiency Test is produced by Ballard and Tighe and is available for assessing students from age 3 through Grade 12 in English and Spanish. It includes listening, speaking, reading, and writing components. Information about it may be found online at www.ballard-tighe.com/products/la/iptFamilyTests.asp.

Language Assessment Scale (LAS)

The Language Assessment Scale Links is produced by CTB/McGraw-Hill for assessing students from preschool through Grade 12. It is available in English and Spanish for students in Grades K–12, and a preschool version is available for children beginning at age 4. It includes listening, speaking, reading, and writing components. Information about it may be found online at www2.ctb.com/sites/laslinks/index.shtml.

WIDA Access Placement Test (W-Apt)

The WIDA Access Placement Test is produced by the WIDA consortium. It is used to identify ELs in Grades K–12 and includes listening, speaking, reading, and writing components. Information about these tests may be found at www.wida.us/assessment/w-apt/index.aspx.

Woodcock-Muñoz Language Survey–Revised (WMLS-R)

The Woodcock-Muñoz may be used with students from preschool through Grade 12 to assess listening, speaking, reading, and writing. It includes English and Spanish versions. Information about it may be found at www.riversidepublishing.com/products/wmls/index.html.

RESOURCE 3.3
Student Oral Language Observation Matrix

Student's Name: _____ Grade: _____ Language: _____

Translator: _____ Date of Observation: _____

Based on your observation of the student, please indicate for each level, with an X in the appropriate box, which best describes the student. Return this matrix to [name of person and position, e.g., Mr. Paxton, School Principal; Mrs. Morales, Director of English Language Education.]

Levels	1	2	3	4	5
A. COMPREHENSION	☐ Cannot be said to understand even simple conversation	☐ Has great difficulty following what is said. Can comprehend only "social conversation" spoken slowly and with frequent repetitions.	☐ Understands most of what is said at slower-than-normal speed with repetitions.	☐ Understands nearly everything at normal speed, although occasional repetition may be necessary.	☐ Understands everyday conversation and normal classroom discussions without difficulty.
B. FLUENCY	☐ Speech is so halting and fragmentary as to make conversation virtually impossible.	☐ Usually hesitant, often forced into silence by language limitations.	☐ Speech in everyday conversation and classroom discussion is frequently disrupted by the student's search for the correct manner of expression.	☐ Speech in everyday conversation and classroom discussions is generally fluent, with occasional lapses while the student searches for the correct manner of expression.	☐ Speech in everyday conversation and classroom discussions is fluent and effortless, approximating that of a native speaker.

Levels	1	2	3	4	5
C. VOCABULARY	☐ Vocabulary limitations are so extreme as to make conversation virtually impossible.	☐ Misuse of words and very limited vocabulary make comprehension quite difficult.	☐ Frequently uses the wrong words. Conversation is somewhat limited because of inadequate vocabulary.	☐ Occasionally uses inappropriate terms and/or must rephrase ideas because of inadequate understanding of vocabulary.	☐ Use of vocabulary and idioms approximates that of a native speaker.
D. PRONUNCIATION	☐ Pronunciation problems are so severe as to make speech virtually unintelligible.	☐ Very hard to understand because of pronunciation problems. Must frequently repeat in order to make self understood.	☐ Pronunciation problems necessitate concentration on the part of the listener and occasionally lead to misunderstanding.	☐ Always intelligible, though one is conscious of a definite accent and occasional inappropriate intonation patterns.	☐ Pronunciation and intonation approximates that of a native speaker.
E. GRAMMAR	☐ Errors in grammar and word order are so severe as to make speech virtually unintelligible.	☐ Grammar and word order errors make comprehension difficult. Must often rephrase and/or restrict self to basic patterns.	☐ Makes frequent errors of grammar and word order, which occasionally obscure meaning.	☐ Occasionally makes grammatical and/or word-order errors, which do not obscure meaning.	☐ Grammatical usage and word order approximate that of a native speaker.

Source: California Department of Education.

RESOURCE 3.4
Identification, Annual, and Transition Assessment

Findings and Recommendations

[Name of District]

Student Name: _____ Gender: M F Grade: _____ Date Tested: _____

Student Assessed By: _____ Position: _____

Assessment Type:

New Student ☐

Annual ☐ _____ #Years in Program [Name of program model type here]

Exit/Transfer From Program ☐

Summary of Listening and Speaking (Include name of the assessment, scores, and summary of findings)

Summary of Reading and Writing (Include name of the assessment, scores, and summary of findings)

Placement Recommendations:

Does not need English language education (ELE) services ☐

Needs ELE services ☐

Reclassify as former EL ☐

ESL level for identified EL (check box that applies)

1 ☐

2 ☐

3 ☐

4 ☐

5 ☐

Clarification in native language needed: No ☐ Yes ☐ Language needed: _____

Description of levels for identified EL:

Level 1: Student is a total beginner and cannot communicate in English at this time.

Student has very limited or no understanding of English and does not use English for communication. He or she responds nonverbally to simple commands, statements, and questions. As oral comprehension increases, will begin to imitate verbalizations of others by using single words or simple phrases. At the earliest stage, constructs meaning from text primarily through illustrations, graphs, maps, and tables.

Level 2: Student understands basic interpersonal conversation when spoken to slowly and with frequent repetition.

Speech is strongly influenced by native language. Student understands phrases and short sentences and can communicate limited information about simple everyday routine situations by using memorized phrases, groups of words, and formulae. Student uses selected simple structures correctly but still systematically produces basic errors. Student is beginning to use general academic vocabulary and familiar everyday expressions. Errors in writing are present that often hinder communication.

Level 3: Student has learned enough vocabulary and language to speak with peers and teachers. However, has not yet developed the competencies in English needed to perform ordinary academic activities.

Student understands more complex speech but still may require some repetition. Student uses English spontaneously but may have difficulty expressing all thoughts due to a restricted vocabulary and limited command of language structure. Student speaks in simple sentences, which are comprehensible and appropriate, but which are frequently marked by grammatical errors. Proficiency in reading may vary considerably. Student is most successful constructing meaning from texts for which he or she has background knowledge upon which to build.

Level 4: Student's language skills are adequate for most day-to-day communication needs. He or she can communicate in English in new or unfamiliar settings but has occasional difficulty with complex structures and abstract academic concepts.

Student may read with considerable fluency and is able to locate and identify the specific facts within the text. However, student may not understand texts in which the concepts are presented in a decontextualized manner, the sentence structure is complex, or the vocabulary is abstract or has multiple meanings. Student can read independently but may have occasional comprehension problems, especially when processing grade-level information.

Level 5: Student has native or near-native use of spoken English. Emphasis is needed on reading and writing with a focus on form and meaning in academic areas.

Student can express himself or herself fluently and spontaneously on a wide range of personal, general, academic, or social topics in a variety of contexts. Student is poised to function in an environment with native-speaking peers with minimal language support or guidance and has a good command of technical and academic vocabulary as well as idiomatic expressions and colloquialisms. Student can produce clear, smoothly flowing, well-structured texts of differing lengths and degrees of linguistic complexity. Errors are minimal, difficult to spot, and generally corrected when they occur.

ESL levels are based on *PreK–12 English Language Proficiency Standards,* published by Teachers of English to Speakers of Other Languages.

RESOURCE 3.5
Interview of Parent/Guardian and/or Newly Identified EL

Newly identified ELs and/or their parents/guardians should be interviewed to assist in building an effective instructional program. The following questions are intended for this purpose. The interview may be conducted with parents/guardians, parents/guardians and their child, or the student. The person conducting the interview should complete this form.

Date of Interview: _____

Student Name: _____ Grade: _____

Interviewer: _____ Position: _____

Who was interviewed: (parent/guardian □, parent/guardian with student □, or student □)

Interpreter (if applicable) _____ Tel: _____

1. How long has [name of student] attended school? _____

   If student has been enrolled in a prior school, ask Questions 2–7. All parents/guardians and/or students should be asked Questions 8–9.

2. What schools has the student attended? Where are these schools located, and what dates did he or she attend?

   School Name: _____

   Location: _____ Dates Attended: _____

   School Name: _____

   Location: _____ Dates Attended: _____

   School Name: _____

   Location: _____ Dates Attended: _____

3. Is more than one language used to communicate in the student's prior schools? Yes □ No □

   If yes, what are the language(s)? Also, please describe when and how these are used.

4. What do classrooms in the student's prior school(s) look like (typical student-teacher ratio, arrangement of desks, print on walls, etc.)? (Try to get a feel for the school.)

5. Please describe the school day (length of day, daily schedule, etc.).

6. What ways do parents/guardians participate in the student's prior school?

7. Were the student's teachers concerned about his or her progress? If yes, please describe the concerns.

8. Do you have any particular concerns, including academic, social, and disciplinary?

9. What is the highest level of education that you and your spouse have completed?

   Elementary ☐

   Middle or Junior High School ☐

   High School or Equivalent ☐

   Community College ☐

   Vocational School ☐

   4-Year College/University ☐

   Professional Graduate Degree ☐

RESOURCE 3.6
School/District Analysis of Its ELs

[District Name]

Note: A separate form should be used for each school in a district. A school may separate these categories further by completing each form by teacher.

Name of School: _____

Languages spoken by the identified ELs: _____

Grade	PK	K	1	2	3	4	5	6	7	8	9	10	11	12

Countries of origin among the identified ELs: _____

Grade	PK	K	1	2	3	4	5	6	7	8	9	10	11	12

English proficiency levels among identified ELs

Grade	PK	K	1	2	3	4	5	6	7	8	9	10	11	12
Level 1														
Level 2														
Level 3														
Level 4														
Level 5														

ELs with interrupted and/or limited prior schooling*

Grade	1	2	3	4	5	6	7	8	9	10	11	12

*Nationally, most students with interrupted prior schooling are provided with specialized programming at the secondary level. However, this information is essential for effective program planning for students in Grades 1–12, and specialized programming should be considered for such students at all grade levels.

ELs on free or reduced lunch*

Grade	PK	K	1	2	3	4	5	6	7	8	9	10	11	12

*This is a general means for identifying students who live in poverty.

ELs receiving Title I services

Grade	PK	K	1	2	3	4	5	6	7	8	9	10	11	12

Highest level of education that parents of ELs completed

Grade	PK	K	1	2	3	4	5	6	7	8	9	10	11	12
Elementary														
Middle School														
High School														
Community College														
4-Year Undergraduate Degree														
Postgraduate Degree														

Teaching ELs

Haynes, J. (2007). *Getting started with English language learners.* Alexandria, VA: Association for Supervision and Curriculum Development.

Haynes, J., & Zacarian, D. (2010). *Teaching English language learners across the content* areas. Alexandria, VA: Association for Supervision and Curriculum Development.

Creating programming for ELs

U.S. Department of Education, Office of Civil Rights. (2005). *Programs for English language learners.* Retrieved December 15, 2010, from http://www2.ed.gov/about/offices/list/ocr/ell/index.html

ELs in general education classroom settings

Faltis, C. (2007). *Teaching English language learners in mainstream classrooms: A joinfostering approach* (4th ed.). New York: Pearson.

Haynes, J., & Zacarian, D. (2010). *Teaching English language learners across the content areas.* Alexandria, VA: Association for Supervision and Curriculum Development.

New Levine, L., & McCloskey, M. (2008). *Teaching English language learners in mainstream classrooms (K–8).* New York: Allyn & Bacon/Merrill.

SIOP model

Echevarria, J., Vogt, M. E., & Short, D. (2004). *Making English comprehensible: Getting started with the SIOP model* (3rd ed.). New York: Pearson.

Planning and implementing bilingual immersion programming

Center for Applied Linguistics. (2010). *Two-way immersion.* Retrieved December 16, 2010, from http://www.cal.org/twi/index.htm

Howard, E. R., & Christian, D. (2002). *Two-way immersion 101: Designing and implementing a two-way immersion program at the elementary level.* Santa Cruz, CA: Center for Research on Education, Diversity and Excellence. Retrieved December 15, 2010, from http://www.cal.org/crede/pdfs/epr9.pdf

Soltero, S. W. (2004). *Dual language: Teaching and learning in two languages.* New York: Pearson.

Teaching students with limited or interrupted prior schooling and students from non-literacy-oriented and culturally disrupted backgrounds

Calderón, M. (2007). *Teaching reading to English language learners 6–12: A framework for improving achievement in content areas.* Thousand Oaks, CA: Corwin.

Calderón, M. E., & Minaya-Rowe, L. (2010). *Preventing long-term ELs: Transforming schools to meet core standards.* Thousand Oaks, CA: Corwin.

Pransky, K. (2008). *Beneath the surface: The hidden realities of teaching culturally and linguistically diverse young learners, K–6.* Portsmouth, NH: Heinemann.

RESOURCE 3.8
Parent Letter About Newly Identified ELs

[District Name]

[School Name]

[School Contact Information]

Date: _____

Dear Parent/Guardian of _____:
                          Name of student

Welcome to [name of school]. Your child was assessed to determine if he or she is an English learner and whether he or she needs a specific program designed to meet his or her English learning needs. Based on these assessments:

1. ☐ Your child appears to be fluent in English and will not require coursework that is designed for students who are learning English as a new language.

2. ☐ It appears that your child is an English learner at the beginning ☐, advanced beginning ☐, early intermediate ☐, intermediate ☐, or transitional level ☐ and would benefit from taking courses that are designed for students who are learning English.

This includes classes in English as a second language. It also includes a course of instruction that is specifically for English learners to be actively engaged in learning content and English. It is recommended that sheltered instruction be provided for your child in math ☐, science ☐, social studies ☐.

Your child would also benefit from receiving bilingual language clarification in math ☐, science ☐, social studies ☐ to assist him or her in understanding subject matter.

You have the right to decline this specifically designed English language education course of study. Please contact me if you have any questions about these recommendations and/or your right to decline. I may be reached at [telephone number] _____.

Thank you.

Sincerely,

[Signature]

[Position]

RESOURCE 3.9
English Language Development Progress Report

[Name of School]

Progress reports are written during the time in which each school completes student progress and report cards. They are intended to provide parents/guardians with information about the progress of their child in learning English.

Student Name: _____ Grade: _____ Academic Year: _____

Teacher: _____ Position: _____ Date: _____

Quarter: 1st Quarter ☐   2nd Quarter ☐   3rd Quarter ☐   4th Quarter ☐

Please rate the student's academic progress in ESL using the code below:

1 = Beginning

2 = Advanced Beginning

3 = Early Intermediate

4 = Intermediate

5 = Transitioning

NA = Not Applicable

	1st Quarter	2nd Quarter	3rd Quarter	4th Quarter

I. Listening/Speaking
    A. One-to-One Interactions
        1. With Peers				

2. With Adults				
B. Small-Group Discussion				
II. Reading A. Reading Comprehension				
B. Reading for Information				
C. Oral Reading				
D. Functional Reading in the Classroom (directions, etc.)				
E. Additional Information About Reading				

	1st Quarter	2nd Quarter	3rd Quarter	4th Quarter
III. Writing A. Functional Writing				
B. Journal Writing				
C. Writing for Reports				
D. Note Taking				
E. Fictional Writing				
F. Additional Information About Writing				

_____ Title I Services _____

_____

_____ Additional Support Services _____

_____

_____ Special Education Services in the Following Areas: _____

_____

Comments/Concerns:

1st Quarter _____

2nd Quarter _____

3rd Quarter _____

4th Quarter _____

RESOURCE 3.10
[School District] Monitor Report

Note: This report deals with students who have been reclassified from EL to former EL.

From: _____ (Position) _____

To: _____

Date student was reclassified: _____ Report Year: 1 ☐ 2 ☐ of two

Student Name: _____ Grade: _____ Academic Year: _____

Teacher: _____ Subject Matter: _____

The above-named student demonstrated the ability to do ordinary classroom work in English and has been reclassified from an *English learner* to a *former English learner*. The student's performance and progress will be monitored for two consecutive school years to assure a successful reclassification. Please rate the student's academic progress in English language arts using the code below:

---

1 = Secure in communicating grade-level concepts and skills

2 = Developing communication in grade-level concepts and skills

3 = Communication is below current grade-level expectations and may need more experiences, support, and time to develop communicative skills and concepts.

+ = Indicates subset is a significant strength relative to overall performance in the subject

− = Indicates subset is a significant weakness relative to overall communicative performance

---

	1st Quarter	2nd Quarter	3rd Quarter	4th Quarter

I. Listening/Speaking
  A. One-to-One Interactions
    1. With Peers				

2. With Adults				
B. Small-Group Discussion				
II. Reading A. Reading Comprehension				
B. Reading for Information				
C. Oral Reading				
D. Functional Reading in the Classroom (directions, etc.)				

	1st Quarter	2nd Quarter	3rd Quarter	4th Quarter
III. Writing A. Functional Writing				
B. Journal Writing				
C. Writing for Reports				
D. Note Taking				
E. Fictional Writing				

_____ Title I _____

_____

_____ Additional Support Services _____

_____

_____ Special Education Services in the Following Areas: _____

_____

Comments/Concerns:

1st Quarter _____

2nd Quarter _____

3rd Quarter _____

4th Quarter _____

REFERENCES

Bailey, F., & Pransky, K. (2005). Are other people's children constructivist learners too? *Theory Into Practice, 44*, 19–26.

Cohen, E., & Lotan, R. (1995). Producing equal-status interactions in the heterogeneous classroom. *American Educational Research Journal, 32*(1), 99–120.

Constantino de Cohen, C., & Clewell, B. (2007). *Putting English language learners on the educational map*. Washington, DC: Urban Institute.

Cummins, J. (2002). Rights and responsibilities of educators of bilingual-bicultural children. In L. D. Soto (Ed.), *Making a difference in the lives of bilingual-bicultural children* (pp. 195–210). New York: Peter Lang.

Delpit, L. (2006). *Other people's children: Cultural conflict in the classroom* (Rev. ed.). New York: New Press.

Faltis, C. (2005). Teaching English language learners in elementary schools: A join-fostering approach (4th ed.). Upper Saddle River, NJ: Prentice Hall.

Gándara, P. (2010). Overcoming triple segregation: Latino students often face language, cultural, and economic isolation. *Educational Leadership, 68*(3), 60–65.

Lindholm-Leary, K. J. (2001). *Dual language education*. Avon, UK: Multilingual Matters.

New York State Department of Education. (2010). Bilingual education. Retrieved December 15, 2010, from http://www.emsc.nysed.gov/biling/bilinged/faq.html

Pransky, K. (2008). *Beneath the surface: The hidden realities of teaching culturally and linguistically diverse young learners K-6*. Portsmouth, NH: Heinemann.

Soltero, S. W. (2004). *Dual language: Teaching and learning in two languages*. New York: Pearson.

U.S. Department of Education. (2004). *Elementary and secondary education, subpart 2, accountability and administration*. Retrieved February 16, 2011, from http://www2.ed.gov/policy/elsec/leg/esea02/pg42.html#sec3121

U.S. Department of Education. (2005). *Developing programs for English language learners: Goals*. Retrieved December 15, 2010, from http://www2.ed.gov/about/offices/list/ocr/ell/goals.html

Zacarian, D. (2007). I can't go to college! *Essential Teacher, 4*(4), 10–11.

4

Designing, Implementing, and/or Strengthening the English as a Second Language Component

Hoa Li was excited to move to the United States. Her family had decided to live near her favorite aunt, uncle, and cousins, who lived in a small city in New England. During her first month in the United States, she and her family lived with their relatives, and she enrolled in the same middle school as her cousins. Because Hoa Li did not speak any English, the school employed a retired English teacher, Mrs. Janus, to work with her for one half hour every day. Mrs. Janus was told to attend Hoa Li's English class and to work with Hoa Li's English teacher, Mr. Lindquist.

Mr. Lindquist asked Mrs. Janus to sit next to Hoa Li and help her understand the novel that his class was reading. Not sure how to do this without interrupting Mr. Lindquist's class, Mrs. Janus silently used her pointer finger to follow along the text as he and Hoa Li's classmates read aloud from it. She had never worked with an English learner (EL), did not speak Mandarin, and didn't want to disturb Mr. Linquist's class. She figured that following along silently was the best solution for Hoa Li. Unfortunately,

Hoa Li did not understand anything that was occurring and felt miserably lost and alone. While Mrs. Janus was worried about disturbing the class, her attempts to help Hoa Li were wholly inadequate.

Two months later, Hoa Li's family found a temporary apartment in another part of the city. At her new school, Hoa Li was placed in an English as a second language[1] (ESL) class for an hour every day. This class met in a small room on the first floor of the school. Hoa Li's schedule required her to attend the first 15 minutes of her grade-level English class, which was on the second floor, leave while the English class was in session, walk to the first floor to attend the ESL class, and then return back to the English class while it was still in session.

Hoa Li found that she was the only Mandarin speaker in the ESL class and that most of her classmates knew a lot more English than she did. She found it difficult to understand the lessons and keep pace with her peers in the ESL class. As she had done in the previous school, she spent most of her time feeling lost and alone. This was even truer when she left her ESL class and attempted to rejoin her English class.

At the end of the semester, her family moved yet again, this time to a more permanent apartment in a different part of the city. Hoa Li's parents, like many parents, did not realize that when they moved, their daughter would be attending a different school. While they were upset that she would be starting out at another new school and concerned about her making another transition, they hoped that Hoa Li would acclimate. Her new school enrolled her in a general English language arts class. Once again, she was unable to follow what occurred in it. She was also assigned to an ESL class. It met for two hours every day during the time that she would have had math and science. In the ESL class, she was surrounded by beginning learners of English like herself. The class was devoted to learning how to speak in English for everyday social conversations. At the end of the school year, Hoa Li's teachers were pleased by how much progress she had made in learning to speak in English. However, Hoa Li and her parents were worried about the math and science courses that she had missed and how behind she was in English language arts.

WHAT IS ENGLISH AS A SECOND LANGUAGE?

ESL describes a type of instruction for learning English. It is often, but not always, taught by an instructor who has been specifically trained to teach English to students who are speakers of other languages at home and are not yet able to do ordinary classroom work in English.

---

[1]The terms *English as a second language* and *English language development* are used interchangeably to describe a type of instruction that is targeted for the learning of English.

Each of the three scenarios that Hoa Li experienced reflects the types of situations in which many of the nation's ELs find themselves. They present an all too familiar dilemma: None addressed the specific English learning needs of students such as Hoa Li. As noted in Chapter 1, there is little uniformity among the amount, type, and effectiveness of ESL instruction that ELs receive. Further, there is often a lack of uniformity and consistency in ESL classes across districts, and even schools within the same district. For example, a beginning learner of English in the third grade might receive an hour of ESL instruction, whereas a fourth grader in the same school might receive two hours and a fifth grader 30 minutes.

This difference was dramatically demonstrated in a survey I conducted of 26 districts in Massachusetts. In some, beginning learners of English received over two and a half hours per day of ESL, while in others, these students received less than a half hour per week! Further, some ESL teachers were relegated to sitting next to the ELs in their regular classrooms and working quietly at the back of the room while the general education teacher conducted a lesson for the whole class. Pull-out ESL classes took students out of general classes such as English, math, science, and social studies as well as during recess and even lunchtime. Most districts reported that the amount of instruction in ESL was not consistent and depended on many variables that had little to do with students' language learning needs, such as the inability of an understaffed ESL program to provide appropriate language services for ELs in all grades, scheduling issues, and space limitations. All in all, each of the school administrators and ESL teacher leaders surveyed reported that they were not able to either schedule or deliver the type of instructional programming that they believed would be the most effective. Programs that are successful must base their programming decisions on the English proficiency levels of students and their learning needs. They must also organize scheduling that allows for the appropriate amount of time for ELs to learn English and subject matter.

In push-in and pull-out settings, ESL and content teachers must also pay focused, intentional, and simultaneous attention to each of four interdependent processes for learning language and content. Drawing from Goldenberg and Coleman (2010), August and Shanahan (2006, 2008), Genesee, Lindholm-Leary, Saunders, and Christian (2006), and Collier (1995), these processes consist of the following and are discussed in more detail in Chapter 5:

- Learning language is a sociocultural process. It involves building connections with ELs' prior personal, social, cultural, and world experiences. It also involves supporting their understanding of the dominant and school cultures.
- Learning language is a developmental process. Teachers must take into account the various proficiency levels of the ELs with whom

they work and target instruction, homework, and assessment to these specific levels.

- Learning language and content occurs best when it builds on the prior academic experiences of students and when the academic and language goals and objectives are made explicit.
- Learning language includes developing a high level of cognitive thinking skills. These must be intentionally taught.

Developing the organizational model of the ESL component of a program

Thus, while the ESL component is a critical element, it must be aligned with these four processes. There is general agreement in the field that there are five to six levels of English proficiency. Teachers of English to Speakers of other Languages (1996–2007) created a five-level set of ESL standards for students in prekindergarten through Grade 12, and the World-Class Instructional Design and Assessment Consortium of 21 states created a six-level format (Board of Regents of the University of Wisconsin System, 2007). Drawing from Haynes and Zacarian (2010), the following describes one way to conceptualize these levels.[2]

Knowing the English proficiency levels and learning needs of students

Stage 1: Starting

This is often referred to as a preproduction stage. Students are not yet able to speak in English with more than one- or two-word responses as they are just beginning to listen in English. Visuals, body language, and activities that are geared for building social vocabulary to navigate the school day are essential. Instructional attention should be focused on building students' listening comprehension through body language, demonstrations, modeling, drawings, and other visuals.

Stage 2: Emerging

This stage usually occurs when students have learned English for six months to a year and are beginning to speak in English, especially in social situations. English is generally learned through visual support and demonstrated by responding to yes/no or either/or questions, naming or categorizing information, and writing very simple sentences to go with pictures.

---

[2]From *Teaching English Language Learners Across the Content Areas* (pp. 10–12), by J. Haynes and D. Zacarian, 2010, Alexandria, VA: ASCD. Copyright 2010 by ASCD. Used with permission. Visit ASCD at www.ascd.org.

Graphic organizers, charts, drawings, demonstrations, and other visuals are essential for learning to occur (Haynes & Zacarian, 2010).

Stage 3: Developing

Students at this stage are beginning to communicate more actively in English using longer and more descriptive sentences. In one to two years, students generally have conversational skills that can be readily used in most social activities. At the same time, the ability to communicate higher-order thinking and academic language in English is just beginning to develop. Students can usually follow simple academic directions, discussions, and tasks when the visual, physical, and *controlled vocabulary* supports are continuously present (Goldenberg & Coleman, 2010). Cummins (1984) describes an important distinction between social and academic language: The ability to speak conversationally in social situations (e.g., during recess, at lunch, on the school bus) usually occurs by Stage 3, but the much-needed and essential academic English language that is needed takes much longer and is representative of Stages 4 and 5. (Refer back to the Chapter 2 discussion of basic interpersonal communication skills versus cognitive academic language proficiency.) Students at Stage 3 require content materials to be modified so that they can be easily accessed through visuals, graphic organizers, and other means by which students can make meaning.

Stage 4: Expanding

Students are becoming more proficient in English at this stage. Generally, they can secure key information in a text, use graphic organizers independently, and skim material for specific information. They are also more able to readily use critical thinking skills to analyze, create, debate, predict, and hypothesize in English. As will be discussed later, literacy-oriented ELs are able to do this with increasing grade-level proficiency and sophistication as their English improves, but non-literacy-oriented and culturally disrupted students are not.

Stage 5: Bridging

Students at this stage are close to being able to perform ordinary classroom work in English. Support may be needed with oral and written use of complex vocabulary, sentence structure, and writing for various purposes and within different academic registers. Students are continuing to learn English. During this important stage, teacher support is needed to fine-tune important grammatical aspects of language and, more essentially, to ensure that students have developed higher-order thinking and communicative skills in English.

In practice, students are much more able to begin to navigate a general academic setting when they are able to communicate in English. This usually occurs when students move from Stage 2 to Stage 3 and beyond. However, as was discussed in Chapters 2 and 3, students from non-literacy-oriented and culturally disrupted backgrounds need much more support and time to develop these skills, and each stage is not equal in terms of the amount of time it takes for students to complete it before moving to the next stage.

The very first step for determining the appropriate ESL model is to review the various English proficiency levels and learning needs of the actual ELs in a school. In Chapter 3, we discussed the importance of taking these steps and a process for doing so. Most students at the beginning stages of learning English are not able to participate meaningfully in a general English language arts classroom. For example, while kindergarten and primary-grade teachers may reasonably believe that there are classroom activities that can be accomplished with students who are at the preproduction stage, these can be made much more possible with the help of an ESL teacher who is familiar with the developmental stages of learning a second language and can help organize the classroom environment and implement tasks and activities that are appropriate for beginning-level ELs. High school English and ESL teachers, on the other hand, may not believe that content can be taught meaningfully to students at the earliest stages in the general classroom even when it is modified, adapted, or taught with in-class support from an ESL teacher. In addition, as we learned in Chapter 2, ELs with limited formal prior education present a unique set of circumstances that must be carefully examined before implementing ESL programming.

Organizing a schedule that allows time to learn English

ESL programming is generally offered in the general classroom (*push-in*) or out of the general classroom (*pull-out*). Whether it is for learning English or for simultaneously learning English and subject matter, the push-in and pull-out models often fail because students receive very little direct and/or comprehensive instruction to learn English (Zacarian, 2009). In the remainder of this chapter, we revisit the three schools that Hoa Li attended so we can look more closely at the models and the organizational structures and resources that are needed for providing the most effective ESL instruction.

A PUSH-IN MODEL

A push-in organizational model of ESL instruction is when ESL is provided in the general education classroom. Usually, it involves an ESL provider going into a general classroom to deliver, support the delivery of, or codeliver instruction. It may include pushing into content area classes such as English, math, science, and social studies. While there are contexts in which to enact a push-in model, it is generally found in elementary schools (DelliCarpini, 2009).

This description of a push-in organizational model alone does not provide school leaders with enough information about the specific structures and organizational approaches that are needed for this model to be effective. For example, in the first school that Hoa Li attended, a retired English teacher, Mrs. Janus, was hired to work with her during a portion of her English class. On the surface, Mrs. Janus provided Hoa Li with additional support every day for 30 minutes. However, Hoa Li did not receive any specific instruction for learning English. Rather, she was expected to learn the language by sitting passively with her peers. Mrs. Janus did not provide Hoa Li with support that was comprehensible or meaningful. Further, Mrs. Janus was not allotted any time to plan with Hoa Li's teacher. Also, it was expected that a half hour a day was enough for Hoa Li to learn English. In this sense, Mrs. Janus was a supporter of the English teacher's program, and the English teacher was responsible for the planning and delivery of it.

While Mrs. Janus might not have been credentialed in ESL, she was hired to provide a push-in model of support ESL. In practice, many ESL teachers are employed to provide this support service. Typically, they work with individual or small groups of students and follow the general education teacher's lead (DelliCarpini, 2009). That is, they do not co-plan with the teacher or deliver the instruction. They often feel relegated to an inferior role and believe that their capacity to deliver quality instruction is disregarded by the general teacher. In these situations, it is also not surprising for the EL to be regarded as inferior as this parallels how the ESL teacher is regarded. The ways in which teachers communicate with students and colleagues greatly reflects the image that we have of our community and society. Cummins (1994) refers to this as the power that teachers have to form the identity and social standing of their students and their colleagues. In the case of Hoa Li, Mrs. Janus was certainly relegated to a position far less important than that of the general English teacher. For all of these reasons, when the ESL model is enacted in this way, it is not likely to be effective.

An additional type of a push-in model occurs when ESL teachers collaboratively plan and deliver instruction with the general education teacher. Both are responsible for the instructional program and take leading roles and responsibilities in implementing it. In these classrooms, according to DelliCarpini (2009), students frequently are not aware of the different roles of their ESL and grade-level teachers. Both teachers value the other as an equal and interdependent partner. In addition, the ESL and general teacher both deliver instruction for the entire time that the subject matter is taught. This method of enacting a push-in model is much more likely to work.

There are many advantages for using a push-in model. It might provide an ideal situation for

- all students to become active members of the class community,
- learning to occur,
- bringing together professionals from different disciplines to create and implement an educational program that is differentiated and individualized for language learning and content learning,
- keeping ELs with English-fluent classmates, and
- creating space where teachers and students become responsible for the learning.

This model can only occur effectively when school leaders provide organizational structures that allow for critical activities. In addition to providing the resources that are needed for the ESL program to work in the general classrooms where it is implemented, professional development and time to co-plan are also required.

A word of caution about push-in models: Research on kindergarten ELs found that separate ESL classes yielded slightly higher performance outcomes (Saunders, Foorman, & Carlson, 2006). And while that study was confined to one grade, it was found to be significant enough to claim that the long-term effect of "separate ESL classes could be substantial" (Goldenberg & Coleman, 2010, p. 78).

Training general education teachers for a push-in model

If a push-in model is the preferred approach, there are several must-dos. In addition to ESL teachers being trained and credentialed to teach ESL, general education teachers must be trained in three critical areas:

1. The principles of second language acquisition that apply to students at different age levels, with a focus on linguistics and the essential role of culture and cultural differences, and the factors that influence successful bilingualism and multiculturalism

2. Methods for delivering effective English instruction to ELs and teaching the four domains of listening, speaking, reading, and writing for the purpose of becoming proficient and literate users of English in school

3. Assessment and evaluation of English learning

Many teacher preparation programs, including those offered by institutions of higher education, educational service agencies, state departments of education, and local schools, do not include this critical element for content teachers of ELs. According to the National Clearinghouse for English

Language Acquisition (NCELA; 2009), only four of the nation's states require teachers of ELs to be trained: California, New York, Arizona, and Florida. Pennsylvania will require this of its teachers by 2011. Seventeen states (Alabama, Colorado, Idaho, Illinois, Iowa, Louisiana, Maryland, Massachusetts, Michigan, Minnesota, Nevada, New Jersey, North Dakota, Rhode Island, Tennessee, Vermont, and Virginia) have requirements for teachers to be "experienced, familiar with and competent" to work with ELs (NCELA, 2009, p. 123). These states offer guidelines for their teachers of ELs and vary widely in terms of what constitutes experience, familiarity, and competency.

Seven states (Alaska, Connecticut, Delaware, Georgia, Kansas, Mississippi, and South Carolina) require their teacher preparation programs to provide curriculum and practical experiences that will prepare teachers for a diverse student population that includes ELs (NCELA, 2009). Eight states (Arkansas, Montana, New Mexico, North Carolina, Ohio, Oregon, West Virginia, and Wyoming) do not refer to ELs or EL pedagogy specifically (NCELA, 2009). Rather, they refer to teacher preparation programs in terms of including curriculum about diversity and not specifically including curriculum for ELs. Fourteen states (Hawaii, Indiana, Kentucky, Maine, Missouri, Nebraska, New Hampshire, Oklahoma, Pennsylvania, South Dakota, Texas, Utah, Washington, and Wisconsin) and the District of Columbia have no requirements.

Teacher preparation requirements, however, do not take into account what is or needs to be occurring for inservice teachers. While teacher preparation programs often serve preservice and inservice teachers, they should not be regarded as the sole means by which teachers will be or are prepared to teach a growing population of ELs. Most classroom teachers have not had training to teach ELs, as seen in Chapter 1. Professional learning to build capacity is a critical need.

To build effective programs for ELs, school leaders must ensure that general content teachers are trained in the three areas noted. A variety of steps can and should be included to ensure that this occurs. First, school leaders should refer to the guidelines of their state department of education to ensure that their school's teachers are appropriately and properly credentialed. Once this occurs, a variety of professional learning models should be explored so that the one that is selected and implemented is the best fit. This may include enrolling general education teachers in programs offered by a local university, the state department of education, or an educational service agency that provide professional development in the three areas noted. Also, school leaders should ensure that they have qualified or, where required, appropriately licensed ESL teachers. In addition, professional learning about collaboration is a must for a push-in model to be highly effective. The term *highly effective* means that teachers have depth of knowledge for achieving student outcomes and that students are successful learners of English and content (Wei, Darling-Hammond, Andree, Richardson, & Orphanos, 2009).

Training ESL teachers to push in content

A push-in model often occurs during content instruction such as math, science, and social studies. Yet many ESL teachers have had no formal training to teach these subjects. In a push-in model, both teachers, content and ESL, must have a solid understanding about content and language learning. In the case of the ESL push-in teacher, content knowledge is essential. ESL teachers require professional development in the following:

- the content curriculum
- the instructional materials that will be used to teach the content
- effective methods for teaching the content

Think of a math class that is focused on quadrilaterals. Instruction of ELs in a push-in classroom must include the efforts of the math and ESL teachers and requires that both have a fundamental understanding of the other's work. Training ESL teachers in content areas is a crucial component for creating an effective push-in model. Teacher preparation, educational service agencies, and others can provide training in content areas. Additionally, many schools can provide peer mentoring and study group formats for this purpose.

Training to collaboratively push in

A push-in model requires teachers to learn how to use a cooperative model of coteaching. It requires a willingness, on the part of teachers and others with whom they work, to work together and co-"do" the right things to achieve the desired outcomes. While universities, educational service agencies, and other institutions offer powerful opportunities for individual teachers to become prepared to teach ELs, a push-in model requires a deepening of thinking about how to do this as a cooperative endeavor. And the model must be specific to the individual students for whom it is implemented and to the school in which this is occurring.

Most important, it must be sustained long enough to transform the culture of the classroom to be a space in which linguistic and cultural diversity is an asset that is part of the core of the curriculum and in which a coteaching model is valued as the most optimal method. Therefore, teacher knowledge about the principles of second language acquisition, methods for teaching ELs, and effective assessment and evaluation of ELs is but one piece of the push-in model. For the model to be employed successfully, it is also critical to study it within the context of a general classroom populated by native speakers of American English as well as ELs.

Implementing a push-in model does not happen by merely putting an ESL teacher in the grade-level or subject matter classroom. It happens when there is a reciprocal and interdependent relationship among the teachers and others who work with students. Professional learning about a push-in model is a must and requires a depth of knowledge on the part of teachers—ESL and grade-level or subject matter alike—about the three core areas discussed earlier as well as a deep sense of and belief in a coteaching model.

An effective push-in model also requires coplanning time for teachers to effectively prepare instruction for an integrated classroom of ELs and monolingual English speakers. Push-in models that work involve school leaders allotting specific and sustained daily or, at the very least, weekly coplanning time.

A PULL-OUT MODEL

Some students are pulled out of general classes to learn in an ESL classroom. Typically, these students spend a scheduled amount of time receiving ESL instruction. Often, but not always, the schedule parallels the student's level of English proficiency whereby Stage 1 (Starting) students spend the longest amount of time in pull-out instruction, and Stage 5 (Bridging) students the least. Figure 3.1 shows a depiction of the pull-out schedule. Each increment represents a prescribed amount of time per day of ESL, such as Starting students receiving 2.5 hours, Emerging students 2 hours, Developing students 1.5 hours, Expanding students 1 hour, and Bridging students .5 hour.

Pull-out ESL models are implemented for a variety of reasons. Some leaders believe them to be more efficient than push-in models. They select a pull-out model as a means of teaching learners from a range of grades and/or general classrooms. This approach is often seen as particularly helpful partly because, on the surface, it provides a way to economically distribute services. An example of this would be an elementary school with four second-grade classrooms, in which the school leader decides to

Figure 4.1 Transitional ESL Pull-Out Model

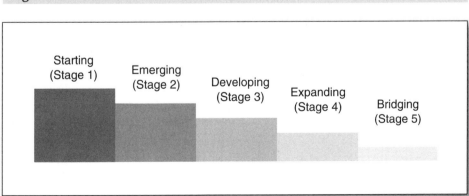

assign ELs to each of these classrooms with the idea that they will leave the classroom for ESL instruction using the type of increments described in Figure 3.1.

For students at the Starting stage, who are just beginning to learn English, a pull-out model may provide the easiest access. It is typical, in these beginning-level classrooms, for students to listen and respond to their teacher's simple commands with appropriate physical movements (e.g., *Go to the door, Open the door, Shut the door*).

In Starting classrooms, students need instruction to help them develop concrete vocabulary words that refer to familiar objects or concrete actions that can be demonstrated by the teacher and acted out by students. Vocabulary is usually introduced in the context in which it is used (e.g., *This is the blackboard, It is lunchtime, Please put your book on the floor, Where is . . . ?*). As students develop more English, they begin to move up the spectrum of proficiency levels. Students at the Developing stage may especially benefit from a pull-out class for the same reasons that students at the Starting stage benefit from it.

Pull-out ESL models are most prevalent at the secondary level (Delli-Carpini, 2009). Students are assigned to ESL classes and generally meet in them for the full class period. Scheduling classes according to proficiency levels at the secondary level may be viewed as a clear way to provide instruction that is specifically tailored to students. Yet inherent in this model are several productive tensions, if not recipes for failure, that must be considered.

ESL pull-out classes work best when they meet during English classes

School leaders should allocate time for ESL during English classes. This allows students much-needed time to learn the language and not miss critical content instruction such as math, science, and social studies. In one of the scenarios presented at the beginning of this chapter, Hoa Li missed her math and science classes to attend her ESL class. This is not a characteristic of an effective program.

Content-based ESL classes work best when they are taught by appropriately credentialed teachers

Content such as science, math, and social studies can be taught while students are learning English. This is often a fine choice as it provides students with instruction that is particularly planned and delivered for learning content and English simultaneously. The Sheltered Instruction Observation Protocol (SIOP; Echeverria, Vogt, & Short, 2007) and Expediting Comprehension for English Language Learners Protocol

(EOP; Calderón, 2007; Calderón & Minaya-Rowe, 2010) are nationally known models that incorporate content and language learning. In classrooms implementing these, teachers must be credentialed to teach content and ESL, meaning that licensed ESL teachers should not be expected to teach math, science, or social studies unless they are credentialed in the subjects and have had the specific training to do so.

Content-based ESL classes should meet during the same time as the content classes for which they are being substituted

Students should not be pulled from one content class, such as math, to an unrelated content class, such as social studies. In content-based ESL classes, ELs should learn the same subject matter as they would have had had they remained in the general classroom. For example, students have ESL in lieu of English, ESL science in lieu of science, and so forth.

Schools must be organized for a smooth exit and reentry to the general education classroom

Students cannot simply leave and reenter a classroom without some thought as to when and how this will occur. As seen in the scenario presented earlier, Hoa Li was required to leave in the midst of her English class and return to it while it was still in session. A first step for organizing the pull-out model is to determine, schoolwide, when students will exit and reenter and how this will occur. This means that teachers of students at various proficiency levels must agree on the time(s) that specific EL students will leave and reenter the classroom. It is not enough to schedule the beginning and ending times of pull-out ESL classes. Teachers must collaborate to create time segments that will work smoothly.

Teachers must collaboratively plan what will occur in general education and ESL classes so that the instructional program is as smooth and seamless as possible

Students need to develop an understanding about what is occurring in the general classroom in order to be participants in it. Pull-out ESL classes can be ideal spaces for students to learn the vocabulary and concepts that are needed. For this to happen, teachers must work collaboratively so that ELs will have as seamless and connected a program as possible. Earlier in this chapter, it was suggested that teachers be trained in how to collaborate. While a pull-out model is not reliant on a coteaching model, it is reliant on each teacher (ESL, grade level, subject matter, and others) having a good grasp of what is occurring in each other's work and building such connections for the benefit of students.

Students should not receive decreasing amounts of ESL as they progress from one stage to the next

The scheduled amount of time for ESL classes should be based on the sufficient amount of instructional time needed for students to matriculate from one stage of acquisition to the next. For example, students at Stage 3 may need the same amount of daily time as those at Stage 1. Further, a transitional model of ESL may not work well for students from non-literacy-oriented and culturally disrupted backgrounds or those with interrupted prior schooling. It is much more ideal to provide ESL for a longer period of time each day (often as much as students in the beginning phases of ESL) to better ensure that literacy development occurs well. This is not to say that Starting learners of English should learn alongside Bridging learners, but students at each of these levels may require the maximum amount of ESL that is possible, such as 2.5 or more hours daily.

Whether a school chooses a push-in or pull-out model, certain things must occur. According to Goldenberg and Coleman (2010), these include the following:

- ESL classes must occur "the moment students walk into the school" (p. 78).
- ESL classes must include a daily focus on listening and speaking in English, direct teaching of English including "vocabulary, syntax, social and conversational conventions, and strategies for how to learn the language" (p. 78).
- Students must be given the opportunity to learn English "authentically and functionally" (p. 78).
- Academic language must be taught across all of the content areas (p. 78).
- Students must be prepared to interact with English-speaking peers (p. 79).

Which model is the one that describes your ESL class? To address our students' needs, we should look at the model that we use to provide ESL and ensure that students are receiving the optimal type and length of instruction. In the next chapter, we will continue to discuss academic programming for ELs, delving more deeply into content instruction and the interdependent connections among the sociocultural, developmental, academic, and cognitive processes of learning language and content.

REFERENCES

August, D., & Shanahan, T. (2006). *Literacy in second language learners: Report of the National Literacy Panel on Language Minority Children and Youth.* Mahwah, NJ: Lawrence Erlbaum.

August, D., & Shanahan, T. (2008). *Developing reading and writing in second language learners: Lessons from a report of the National Literacy Panel on Language Minority Children and Youth.* New York: Routledge.

Board of Regents of the University of Wisconsin System. (2007). *English language proficiency (ELP) standards.* Retrieved December 18, 2010, from http://www .wida.us/standards/CAN_DOs.pdf

Calderón, M. (2007). *Teaching reading to English language learners 6–12: A framework for improving achievement in content areas.* Thousand Oaks, CA: Corwin.

Calderón, M. E., & Minaya-Rowe, L. (2010). Preventing long-term ELs: Transforming schools to meet core standards. Thousand Oaks, CA: Corwin.

Collier, V. (1995). Acquiring a second language for school. Directions in Language and Education, *1*(4). Retrieved December 18, 2010, from http:// www.eric.ed.gov/ERICWebPortal/detail?accno=ED394301

Cummins, J. (1984). *Bilingualism and special education: Issues in assessment and pedagogy.* Clevedon, UK: Multilingual Matters.

Cummins, J. (1994). Knowledge, power, and identity in teaching English as a second language. In F. Genesee (Ed.), *Educating second language children: The whole child, the whole curriculum, the whole community* (pp. 33–58). New York: Cambridge University Press.

DelliCarpini, M. (2009). Dialogues across disciplines: Preparing English-as-a-second-language teachers for interdisciplinary collaboration. *Current Issues in Education, 11*(2). Retrieved December 18, 2010, from http://cie.ed.asu.edu/volume11/number2/

Echevarria, J. A., Vogt, M. E., & Short, D. J. (2007). *Making content comprehensible for English learners: The SIOP model* (3rd ed.). Boston: Allyn & Bacon.

Genesee, F., Lindholm-Leary, K., Saunders, W., & Christian, D. (2006). *Educating English language learners.* New York: Cambridge University Press.

Goldenberg, C., & Coleman, R. (2010). *Promoting academic achievement among English learners: A guide to the research.* Thousand Oaks, CA: Corwin.

Haynes, J., & Zacarian, D. (2010). Teaching content to English language learners. Alexandria, VA: Association for Supervision and Curriculum Development.

National Clearinghouse for English Language Acquisition. (2009). *Educating English language learners: Building teacher capacity, round table report: Volume II, annotated bibliography.* Retrieved December 18, 2010, from http://www.ncela .gwu.edu/files/uploads/3/EducatingELLsBuildingTeacherCapacityVol2 .pdf

Saunders, W., Foorman, B., & Carlson, C. (2006). Do we need a separate block of time for oral English language development in program for English learners? *Elementary School Journal, 107,* 181–198.

Teachers of English to Speakers of Other Languages. (1996–2007). *PreK–12 English language proficiency standards framework.* Retrieved December 18, 2010, from http://www.tesol.org/s_tesol/sec_document.asp?CID=281&DID=13323

Wei, R. C., Darling-Hammond, L., Andree, A., Richardson, N., & Orphanos, S. (2009). *Professional learning in the learning profession: A status report on teacher development in the United States and abroad.* Dallas, TX: National Staff Development Council.

Zacarian, D. (2009). How long should ESL classes be? And why? *Essential Teacher, 6*(3/4), 10–11.

5

Addressing the Subject Matter Component of an English Language Education Program

"What did you notice about your group's work?" Mr. Rodriguez, a high school math teacher, asked his students.

"We understood what Antonio shared with us, and he helped us create a null hypothesis," a student from one of the small groups responded.

"How did you communicate with Antonio? Did you speak in Portuguese?" Mr. Rodriguez asked them.

"Yes and no," they responded.

"While Daniel helped Antonio because he can speak Portuguese, we also listened carefully to your question and used paper to talk through our responses," responded Claire, one of Antonio's teammates. "Having Antonio be the group's illustrator really helped us."

"And what did you learn?" Mr. Rodriguez asked. Marta, another group member, answered the question by saying that the group was able to create their null hypothesis by observing Antonio draw their hypothesis on paper.

"And what is your null hypothesis?" Mr. Rodriguez asked.

"Our hypothesis," Marta answered, "is that English learners are not included in advanced placement courses and that this is not due to chance." Listening carefully to the small group's response, Mr. Rodriguez noted their null hypothesis and talked about the group's work.

He asked each of the six small cooperative learning groups in his math class to make note of how many times each member of the group contributed. To model what he meant by "contributed," he did a think-aloud and suggested one type of contribution. "Let me think about what would be a contribution. I have an idea. If you notice that one member of your group states a way to collect data, this could be called a *contribution*. Let me write this on the board. What else might we consider as a contribution to creating a null hypothesis?" Mr. Rodriguez asked as he wrote "States a way to collect data."

Some suggested that "drawing it out" was a contribution and referenced Antonio. Others suggested that a contribution was when a teammate pointed to or shared specific pages in the course text to help solve the problem. One group's members whispered to each other and pointed to their spokesperson, who said, "A contribution is when we learn from what's written on the board."

Mr. Rodriguez then suggested that they create a matrix of acceptable contributions. At the end of five minutes, the class had created a list of four acceptable contributions. Table 5.1 illustrates the chart that Mr. Rodriguez and his class created for tallying all of the contributions. Mr. Rodriguez then asked one member of each small group to make a tally sheet of that group's contributions. "It will help us in knowing that everyone has something to contribute to our class," he told them.

Antonio's small group of four began working on determining the ways in which they would collect data to test their null hypothesis. Mr. Rodriguez noted that they leaned forward to the center of their table to watch Antonio draw on a piece of chart paper. He observed one of the members pointing to the board and talking about the problem while also pointing to what Antonio had written.

Table 5.1   Contribution Tally Sheet for Problem Set Solutions

	Drawing	Saying an Answer or Suggestion	Suggesting a Page From the Course Text	Suggesting an Example From the Board
Antonio	///			
Thomas		///// /////		//
Marta		/////	//	/////
Claire		///// ////	///	/////

While Mr. Rodriguez was walking around the classroom and observing his students' response to the problem set, Ms. Brown, the school principal, dropped into his class. She observed that three objectives had been written on the board. The first was listed as an overarching objective. It stated: "How is math used to make predictions about our lives?" The second was listed as the day's learning objective and stated: "Today, we will be able to solve a problem using a statistical hypothesis test." The third was stated as the day's language objectives that students would do:

1. In small groups, we will create a null hypothesis problem.

2. In small groups, we will create a means for collecting data to test our null hypothesis.

3. We will track our small group's contributions to the creation of our null hypothesis.

4. We will share our data collection plans with another small group.

Ms. Brown also observed several problem sets displayed on the board, above which was a list of vocabulary about the topic of null hypothesis that Mr. Rodriguez and his students had created. The list was separated into categories and was accompanied by student-generated drawings of their meaning. Ms. Brown also observed that there was a *tally keeper* in each small group who was marking down the type of contribution that each peer was making. She noted that Antonio and other English learners (ELs) in the class were contributing in ways that she had not expected, including the way in which Antonio was illustrating the math problem. Before waving goodbye to Mr. Rodriguez and his class as she prepared to drop into another math class, Ms. Brown whispered to Mr. Rodriguez, 'Your students are so engaged. What are you doing to keep them on task and make your lesson so effective?"

What did Mr. Rodriguez do to make his lesson meaningful and effective?

In this chapter, we will discuss the various steps that should be involved in teaching content to ELs. The intent is to share how content lessons should be taught so that all learners have access to learning.

WHAT CONSTITUTES A HIGH-QUALITY CONTENT LESSON FOR AN EL?

This section presents eight principles for providing high-quality content lessons. These relate to the four interdependent processes of language and content learning introduced in Chapter 4 and drawn from Goldenberg and Coleman (2010); August and Shanahan (2006, 2008); Genesee, Lindholm-Leary, Saunders, and Christian (2006); and Collier (1995). Each principle is important to include, whether the language of instruction is the student's primary language, English with support in the student's native language, or solely English. In addition, these principles apply in settings composed of ELs only, ELs and native speakers of English, and students with interrupted formal education. Indeed, these principles apply to all settings where ELs are instructed.

Learning is a sociocultural process

Principle 1: Connect academic learning to socially relevant issues that are personal to students' lives

High-quality lessons must be connected to students' lives in a way that propels and compels students' interest to learn content. Building connections is not as simple as connecting content to what students have learned in the classroom. Rather, learning is a social endeavor that requires a high level of interaction and connection making. It means taking time to learn what students already know and using this information to support the learning of new information in an interactive environment (Bandura, 1977). Taking time to learn about students may seem like a daunting task given the number of students that teachers teach and their diverse cultural and language experiences. However, this should not be considered a barrier that cannot be addressed. Selecting issues that are socially relevant for students can be a very effective means for building student interest to study content. It helps to take something that is important to students and connect it with something that may seem entirely irrelevant or unobtainable.

Connecting curriculum with socially relevant issues provides a means for getting students interested in learning content because it helps the task of learning to be personally connected (Vasquez, 2010). For example, a course in U.S. history may be made more easily relevant for a U.S.-born speaker of English than it would an EL who was born and spent his or her primary years in a nondemocratic country. In the United States, for example, the civil rights work of Martin Luther King Jr. is honored in a number of ways, including celebrating his birth as a national holiday on the third Monday of every January. Many children learn about King and the civil rights movement in preschool, before they enter grade school. Thus, a lesson about this topic may be more easily understood and valued by native speakers of English from the United States than others because of the background knowledge that has been built up since they were very young children. Finding value in learning about U.S. history has to be connected to something that is relevant to every student's life, including students who are not from the United States or familiar with its history. The absence of these connections can literally disconnect students from the learning process. This is especially true for ELs and other students who find learning to be challenging.

Gus Lee, award-winning author of *China Boy* (1991), has talked about his desire to drop out of school and become a gang member (2000). When he enrolled in the ninth grade and attended the first day of his English class, his teacher told the class that they would be reading the book *Pride and Prejudice* throughout the year. The book, written in 1813 by Jane Austen, a woman who wrote romantic novels set in upper-class settings in England, had little relevance to Lee's life as a Chinese American. Convinced that school was not for him, he went to his English teacher to tell her that he would soon be dropping out of school. His teacher asked Lee what he knew about pride, and when he did not respond, she then asked him what he knew about prejudice. He knew quite a bit and responded to the question. When she told him that they would be learning about prejudice throughout the year and that his personal experience with it would be important, it compelled him to do more than just take the English course; he stayed in school and later developed an illustrious career as an assistant attorney general, author, and featured speaker. Lee's teacher helped him find value in learning the content, an important key principle. Effective lessons should include connections to something that is socially relevant while supporting the learning of content.

Mr. Rodriguez, the high school math teacher referenced at the beginning of this chapter, needed to think about math in terms of his students' lives to make it have value. He found a copy of a study about racial and gender profiling (*Massachusetts Racial and Gender Profiling Technical Report*, 2004) and brought it to class. The report, he hoped, would help spark student interest in learning math. It provided information about traffic violations by race and gender and included the towns and cities in which these had occurred. Drawing from a mathematics unit created by William Blatner (2006), Mr. Rodriguez selected this study because he knew that most of his students were reaching an age at which they would soon be obtaining a driver's license. He selected specific parts of the study and posed the following question: *Do you think that students of color from our town will have a higher chance of receiving a traffic violation than white people?* He selected this question because of its socially just relevance and a belief that learning involves creating a space in which students can discuss social issues that are relevant to them. Drawing from the study, each small group looked at the data and drew various conclusions. After this examination, Mr. Rodriguez asked his students to create a hypothesis that would examine the disparities that they thought existed in their personal lives through conducting a mathematical analysis of them.

With data gathered from the school principal, the small group that hypothesized that "there was no difference between the proportion of ELs in honors classes and the proportion of ELs expected to be in honor classes" conducted a computer simulation of their null hypothesis. They found that the actual proportion of ELs in honors classes occurred less than 4 times in 1,000 simulated trials and concluded that it was highly unlikely that the situation in their school had occurred by chance.

Mr. Rodriguez found that his students eagerly engaged in their small-group projects. Everyone, including the group that examined the honors classes, examined a socially relevant issue. Mr. Rodriguez went a step further. He encouraged his students to present their findings to their classmates and others, including school administrators.

Connecting curriculum to socially and personally relevant issues creates student interest in learning. It helps to move content from being dry and rote to being of interest and value to students. There are limitless ideas for making content relevant. When teachers take time to seek ways to do this, all students, including ELs, are more compelled to learn.

Principle 2: Build background knowledge by activating prior knowledge

In addition to helping students find value in learning, building background should include four means for activating prior knowledge with content: students' prior personal, social, cultural, and world experiences.

Connecting content to students' prior experiences can be accomplished in a myriad of ways. Drawing from ideas about how the brain works, connecting content to a student's personal experiences is an important key for connecting what a student knows to what is not known (Caine & Caine, 1991; Caine, Caine, McClintic, & Klimek, 2005; Sylwester & Cho, 1992). A powerful example of activating ELs' prior knowledge can be found in the Sheltered Instruction Observation Protocol (SIOP; Echevarria, Vogt, & Short, 2002), a lesson planning and delivery model for ELs. In a video that is a companion to texts on the SIOP model (Hubec & Short, 2002), a teacher delivers a lesson about the time in which early European settlers moved to the United States. A large course text can be seen, as can various facts about and maps of this historical time period. To activate her students' knowledge, the teacher asks them a question about their personal experiences: "List the reasons why you and your family or someone you know came to the United States." Thus, while the text and maps are filled with historical facts, the teacher wisely chooses a means for connecting her students' experiences to key content and concept ideas.

A good rule of thumb is to build these types of background connections in the beginning of a unit so that, in addition to creating lessons that are socially relevant to students' lives, building connections to students' personal, social, cultural, and educational experiences accentuates making learning meaningful and comprehensible.

Principle 3: Use cooperative learning

Cooperative learning should be a mainstay in any classroom with ELs. The small interactive space of pair and small-group work provides students with multiple practice opportunities to use, apply, and learn the language of content (Calderón & Minaya-Rowe, 2010; Cohen, 1994; Haynes & Zacarian, 2010; Johnson & Johnson, 1985; Johnson, Johnson, &

Johnson Holubec, 1986). Pair and group work should occur after the teacher has introduced the overarching unit objective and the day's content and language objectives. It should also occur after the teacher has provided a model for enacting the type of pair and group work that is assigned. For example, after Mr. Rodriguez displayed and shared his overarching objective and the day's content and language objectives, he provided his students with an example, a model and think-aloud, of what constituted a contribution for the group's task. He included a visual display of the vocabulary that he needed to form a mathematical hypothesis. He did this so that his students could see the type of response that he was seeking and have the vocabulary readily available. Providing a model, or think-aloud, is not the only means of engaging students to learn cooperatively and will not necessarily yield the outcomes that are desired.

Group work is a complex endeavor. It involves teachers reducing their authority and control for students to learn with and from each other (Cohen, 1994; Zacarian, 1996). The rules of engaging in group work are often implied. Think of a teacher who instructs students to "get in their groups" or "talk with a partner." These seemingly simple directions have many hidden expectations, including that students will know what is expected of them when they work in groups—namely, that they will work collegially and participate evenly and equitably. In addition, roles are often not assigned and students are expected to simply work together.

When teachers take time to help their students learn about and work on the *process* of pair and group work and administrators support this activity, learning is much more likely to occur among all participants (Zacarian, 1996). Mr. Rodriguez, for example, assigned roles to each member of the group and engaged the groups in taking a tally of the types of responses that each participant contributed to the group's process. These activities, assigning roles and noting a group's communication process, helped to promote the effectiveness of the group work model.

For many reasons, ELs are not as likely to contribute to group or pair work as their peers. They may not yet have the capacity to speak in English with fluency because they may be at a stage of language learning where they are translating ideas from English to their native language in order to comprehend them. In addition, many ELs may be afraid to make errors in front of peers, and the pace of conversation may be too fast for ELs to keep up with. Also, the group's talk may reflect personal, world, or cultural experiences with which ELs are not familiar. Each of these challenges can be addressed when teachers take time to manage the process of group or pair work.

A first and important step is to assign roles that parallel the English proficiency levels of the ELs in the group. Mr. Rodriguez, for example, assigned the role of artist to the ELs who were at a stage of English proficiency that matched this role. Many different roles can support pair and group work, including listener, illustrator, and "ask the teacher." In addition to assigning roles, teachers must take time to explain how roles will be enacted. A second step is to help the group in its interactive process. This may be done in a myriad of ways, including coming to agreement about the types of contributions that count as participation and having a member of the group make note of them. It may include having partners or groups reflect on their work together and make note of its strengths and what needs to occur. It may also include creating a matrix for group process and having groups self-grade their process of collaborative work. Pair and group work involves two functions: process and product. Mr. Rodriguez asked each group to note their contributions to the group's task. This is a process function. Creating a null hypothesis is a task or product function.

Cooperative learning is an important element in an effective lesson. When it incorporates assigning roles, matching tasks and activities to the level of ELs' proficiency in English, and paying attention to group process and group product, it can be a powerful teaching method.

Learning is a developmental process

Principle 4: Deliver lessons that are comprehensible

In an era of high-stakes testing in which high school graduation depends on students passing state exams, many teachers may feel pressured to cover all of the curriculum and to "teach to the test." This can lead to surface coverage of content and a desire to teach as quickly as possible to cover it all. ELs are not able to grasp fast-paced lessons delivered in English as they are learning English and content simultaneously. The quickness of the pace can become an even larger challenge for students with limited or interrupted prior schooling or schooling that does not match that of an American public school. This is true whether the lesson is delivered in English or in a student's native language.

Making lessons comprehensible means making them understandable. Teachers must factor in the pace of the lesson as well as the volume of text that is required for students to learn content. Mr. Rodriguez was careful to speak slowly and carefully as he delivered his lesson. He also deliberately provided ample practice space when his students worked in small groups. And he required his students to take a tally of who was contributing as a means of ensuring that every student was contributing actively. The means for receiving a tally mark included a wide variety of communicative tasks that matched his ELs' level of English proficiency. Thus, whether he was teaching the lesson or his students were engaging in group work related to it, the pace of the class deliberately and intentionally took into account the ELs in his classroom as well as the students with varying learning styles and differences.

Knowing the English proficiency levels of ELs and creating tasks and activities that parallel these levels is essential. Equally important is considering the use of students' native languages and providing students with opportunities to use their native languages for learning (Gebhard, 2002/2003). Mr. Rodriguez, for example, knew that Antonio was just beginning the third stage of learning English, where he would be able to communicate more actively in English. He knew that Antonio would be more comfortable drawing and illustrating his ideas using a limited amount of written English rather than attempting to write his mathematical ideas solely in English. Mr. Rodriguez also knew that it was perfectly fine for Antonio to express his ideas in Portuguese, and he encouraged him to do so with a fellow classmate. When Antonio engaged in class, his drawings conveyed his ideas and were a way for Mr. Rodriguez to know that Antonio understood the lesson.

Since Mr. Rodriguez frequently used group work, he also created ways in which the lesson would be made more comprehensible when ELs worked with peers. For example, he made sure to place Antonio in a group with a peer who spoke Portuguese. He also encouraged the group to use drawings to help Antonio understand their ideas with meaning. The importance of making lessons comprehensible goes beyond looking at what is stated by a teacher to what is done by students in order to use the language of content.

In addition, when Mr. Rodriguez assigned homework to Antonio, he made sure that it involved tasks that Antonio had done successfully in class. While Antonio was able to write and solve mathematical formulas using numbers, he was not able to express these in English in a written format. Mr. Rodriguez assigned Antonio homework that required him to use English at his level of proficiency. Designing lessons for understanding must take into account factors such as these.

Principle 5: Modify assessments and homework

ELs are engaged in learning English as they are learning content. Unlike peers who are fluent in English, they must engage in both of these processes simultaneously. Homework and assessments can be particularly challenging for ELs. This is especially true in classrooms that do not make accommodations or modifications. The English proficiency level of a student is key for determining appropriate tasks and assignments. ELs should be assigned tasks and activities that are just a little beyond their level of English proficiency (Krashen, 2002). Some may argue that this means doing less and "dumbing down" the instructional program and teachers' expectations of students. Actually, it means creatively thinking about what is possible for students to do to demonstrate understanding, and creating tasks that match it. For example, Mr. Rodriguez assigned the role of illustrator to Antonio and some of the other students. Their mathematical illustrations of a null hypothesis provided him with clear evidence that they had learned and understood the concepts. Thus the assignment ("work in groups to create a null hypothesis") was enacted through a variety of roles that Mr. Rodriguez assigned, including one that he, the ELs, and their peers could assess as it was occurring. Observing the illustration role as it was occurring provided Mr. Rodriguez with an on-the-spot means of assessing students. The end-of-unit summative assessments were also based on their levels of English proficiency. Thus, the formative on-the-spot and summative assessments were designed and delivered to match his ELs' level of English.

Homework is often too challenging for ELs to complete successfully. All too often, teachers assign the same homework to ELs as they do to everyone else in the class. There is an expectation that homework can be completed independently when, in reality, ELs need, if not depend on, guided practice opportunities that are continuously furnished by their teachers and peers. Differentiating homework tasks is critical for ensuring that ELs not only can do the homework but will not find it too difficult or impossible to accomplish. Differentiating homework tasks and assignments is essential. They must match students' English proficiency level and their level of content understanding.

How can teachers assign homework for ELs? An important rule of thumb is to design homework that is based on the principles presented in this chapter. Each of these implies that teachers will differentiate instruction to match the individual needs of their students. Homework is completed during a time in which students are out of class and on their own. Teachers should think about the types of tasks that their ELs are able to complete successfully in class and extend these as homework assignments. Illustrating another hypothesis may be an appropriate homework assignment for Mr. Rodriguez's ELs, for example. Homework tasks that are way beyond a student's level of comprehension can lead to disengagement of students (Vatterott, 2009). Differentiation should consider the following:

1. The amount of work assigned. Teachers must think carefully about the amount of time that is needed for each EL to complete the assignment, then assign tasks that will not take an inordinate amount. One task may take an English-fluent student a few minutes and an EL over an hour. Thinking this through carefully is important.

2. The type of work assigned. Simpler or modified reading and writing tasks are more appropriate for some ELs, as are adapted texts. These give students much-needed time to learn material that is not overwhelming.

3. Organizing homework for ELs. ELs continue to need visual displays to do out-of-class assignments. The overarching content and learning objectives, key vocabulary, and graphic organizers that are used in class, for example, are key supports for students at home (Haynes & Zacarian, 2010).

4. Feedback from students about the homework that is assigned. Asking students for feedback about their homework experience can be a critical means for assessing its effectiveness. Teachers can ask questions such as the following:

I was able to understand the homework assignment because ____
_____.

I found the homework to be too difficult because I didn't understand the following: _____.

The homework helped me learn _____.

Learning is academic

Principle 6: Define overarching objectives
and the day's learning and language objectives

An important principle for making lessons effective is to determine (1) the key content concepts that are essential for students to learn and (2) what they will need to do to learn these key concepts. Gardner (2009) outlines specific abilities that are needed by leaders. One is the ability to take a mass of information, sort through it, determine the key information that is important, and convey it succinctly to others. Teachers are leaders of their classrooms. They are also the deliverers of content. Some content, such as a high school biology or history text, is dense and filled with information. Other content, such as a picture book used to teach kindergarten students how to read, contains illustrations and other graphics that do not necessarily depict the key idea that is important for students to learn. Teachers have an important role in considering what it is they want students to learn and then conveying this to them. Teachers must also provide their students, especially ELs, with access to the content.

Displaying an overarching unit objective is an important first step to making the key content visible (Haynes & Zacarian, 2010; Wiggins & McTighe, 2005). Mr. Rodriguez posted an overarching unit objective on the board: "How is math used to make predictions about our lives?" Writing this in the form of a question was intended to pique his students' interest in solving the question. The overarching question remained on the board throughout the unit of study. Each lesson began and ended with Mr. Rodriguez referring to the overarching unit question. The reason that he displayed this unit objective was to help his students focus on the content to be learned. The presence of an overarching question is an important principle of an effective lesson.

Displaying the day's learning objective is also important (Echevarria et al., 2002; Haynes & Zacarian, 2010). It provides a clear idea of what is to be learned and plays an important role in helping students understand the various functions of language, such as using language to hypothesize.

For example, Mr. Rodriguez posted this learning objective: "Today, we will be able to solve a problem by using a statistical hypothesis test." He spent time thinking about the content that his students would learn and created this single learning objective for the day's lesson. Many teachers draw from their state and local curriculum standards to design and deliver lessons. These are generally written in teacher language; that is, the standards are written in educational language that is not student friendly. A good content objective must be written in student-friendly, age-appropriate language. However, a learning objective is not enough to help all learners.

As part of a print-rich environment, short statements about what students will do in order to learn are important to include in the day's objectives. Echevarria et al. (2002) describe these as language objectives. It is important to think of these as how students will communicate to use the language of content or what they will do to listen, speak, read, and write during the lesson.

Mr. Rodriguez listed four language objectives for the day's lesson: (1) In small groups, we will create a null hypothesis problem; (2) We will create a means for collecting data to test it; (3) We will track our small group's contributions to creating our null hypothesis; (4) We will then share our null hypothesis and data collection plans with another small group for feedback.

An overarching unit objective as well as daily content and language objectives are critical to designing and delivering effective content lessons.

Principle 7: Target vocabulary instruction

Haynes and Zacarian (2010) refer to vocabulary as the terms, words, idioms, and phrases (TWIPs) that students need to learn and use. Beck, McKoewen, and Kucan (2002) provide a way for leaders to think about vocabulary in terms of three tiers, or levels. Drawing from Haynes and Zacarian and Beck et al., Tier 1 TWIPs reflect common basic one- to two-syllable words or phrases that are typically and frequently used in everyday conversation (e.g., *couch, pencil, chair, school, walk*). While many believe that these are not necessary to teach because of their frequency of use, they are a must for beginning speakers of English. As seen in Chapter 2, teachers of preproduction and emerging learners of English must provide instruction of Tier 1 words. Teaching this level of words is often accompanied with visuals such as labeling the classroom and creating flash cards. In addition, teachers will often act out the words using body language and kinesthetic displays to help students use these common everyday words through experiential learning. All ELs need intentional support to learn common every day TWIPs, especially those with multiple meanings: anaphoric references to replace words or phrases (e.g., *The test was delayed. It was put off.*) and idiomatic expressions (e.g., *put up, put down, put off*).

Content vocabulary is essential for students. Tier 3 TWIPs are unlike those at Tier 1 in that they are not used with high frequency. Indeed, they are used infrequently and are often multisyllabic (Beck et al., 2002). Terms such as *quadratic equation, null hypothesis, hexagon, barometric pressure,* and *iambic pentameter* are examples of Tier 3 TWIPs. They are also academic terms that are not likely to be used outside of the classroom in which the content is being taught. ELs and others need to be taught these words for them to "stick." However, unlike fluent speakers of English, ELs need as many as 20 practice opportunities using these TWIPs in context to learn them (Calderón, 2009; Hinkel, 2009). Mr. Rodriguez posted a word wall of Tier 3 mathematical vocabulary that was essential for his students to learn. Marzano (2010) conducted a study of the academic vocabulary that is needed by most students. While content books are filled with content-specific vocabulary, much less is actually needed and used by students. This is quite important to consider when planning and delivering lessons. For example, prior to teaching the lesson, Mr. Rodriguez reviewed all of the math vocabulary that was used in the course text on the topic of null hypothesis and selected the key terms that he believed were essential for his students. In other words, Tier 3 words must be taught to be learned, but it is important to synthesize the key vocabulary that is essential for content learning and peel away what is not. Visuals such as student drawings of the vocabulary (Marzano & Pickering, 2005) and word walls that are sorted by categories (Haynes & Zacarian, 2010), as well as student practice using the vocabulary in context, are essential for learning content vocabulary.

However, everyday basic vocabulary and content vocabulary are not all that students need. Indeed, there is a large volume of other words, those at Tier 2, that are needed to be successful in school. According to Beck et al. (2002), Tier 2 vocabulary refers to synonyms for Tier 1 words. Tier 2 vocabulary is much more specific and descriptive than Tier 1 vocabulary and is often one or two syllables longer than Tier 1 words (e.g., *sofa, love seat, divan*). Tier 2 also includes transition words that are used to mean *and, but,* and *so* and include words such as *also, however,* and *therefore.* These are essential not just for the English language development of ELs but for all students.

ELs with well-developed vocabularies in their first language are likely to be able to transfer these vocabulary skills into their second language. Students with large Tier 2 first-language vocabularies are generally from literacy-oriented backgrounds (Pransky, 2008; Pransky & Zacarian 2011). Students who do not have well-developed Tier 2 vocabularies in their native language, including students with limited or interrupted prior schooling, need focused and continuous instruction on this tier. Developing Tier 2 vocabulary should be part of the instructional program of any English language development and content teacher. Unlike Tier 1 words, which occur in high frequency in everyday conversation, Tier 2 words are less likely to be used unless they are directly taught to students and students are provided with multiple practice opportunities to use these in listening, speaking, reading, and writing contexts (Calderón, 2007; Pransky & Zacarian, 2011). Words walls, handouts, and other visual displays are essential for this type of vocabulary development.

It is important to note that students with interrupted schooling and those from non-literacy-oriented homes and/or culturally disrupted backgrounds may need a more intensive form of vocabulary development. Margarita Calderón (2007) addresses the need for teachers to focus academic instruction intentionally and purposefully in key areas, including students' word knowledge, reading fluency, understanding of classroom texts, discussion skills, grammar knowledge and use, writing skills, and spelling. Building word knowledge should be the heart of any academic program for ELs. According to Calderón, comprehension depends on a student knowing 90% to 95% of the words in a text. To support vocabulary learning, she emphasizes the importance of a teacher saying the word aloud, asking students to repeat it three times, providing students with examples of the word in context with content text, supporting dictionary definitions with those that have student-friendly wording, and engaging students in multiple practice opportunities to use the word in context.

Learning is a cognitive process

Principle 8: Thinking skills must be
explicitly taught and visually displayed

Language is used to convey our thoughts. Whether we use language to listen, speak, read, or write, each of these domains is a means for communicating what we are thinking. School is an environment in which students are expected to use a high level of thinking and cognitive skills. Bloom's Taxonomy is a helpful means for understanding the types of thinking skills that students need (Anderson & Krathwohl, 2001; Bloom & Krathwohl, 1956). These fall into six categories of increasing levels of complexity:

- remembering
- understanding
- applying
- analyzing
- evaluating
- creating

Mr. Rodriguez required his students to create a null hypothesis, a task that required the very highest level of cognition. His students needed to *remember* information about what a null hypothesis was. They needed to *understand* what this definition meant and what it did not mean. They needed to *apply* the definition to engage in the assigned task. They needed to *analyze* and *evaluate* the means by which they would measure their null hypothesis. They also needed to *create* the null hypothesis, the most complex of the six categories listed above. The means by which these thinking skills are taught are critical. Mr. Rodriguez modeled aloud the thinking skills that were needed. It is important for teachers to identify the thinking skills that students need and to explicitly teach them. These may include such important skills as the following:

Clarify	Explain	Predict
Consider	Hypothesize	Report
Convince	Illustrate	Request
Create	Imagine	Respond
Describe	Infer	Retell
Direct	Interact	Summarize
Draw	Persuade	Synthesize

Each one of these requires a different type of thinking skill. What is critical is that each be identified and explicitly taught so that every student has the opportunity to learn what each word means in practice.

Using visuals

Visual displays are important for delivering high-quality lessons. Along with visibly displaying the overarching unit objective and the day's learning and language objectives, graphic organizers and pictures that include maps, drawings, photographs, graphs, and charts should also be included. Visuals provide an important means for the brain to "see," or grasp, ideas and concepts (Jensen, 2005; Hyerle, Curtis, & Alper, 2004).

Authentic visuals such as videos, photographs, and drawings of a concept provide helpful access for learning. Field trips to locations where the concept can be seen (e.g., a walking trip to the local post office to see the process of sending and receiving a letter) is a great way to make lessons authentic because students experience the context in which the concept occurs. Conducting these at the beginning of a unit (as opposed to as a culminating activity at the conclusion) is a very helpful way for making the content understandable by situating students in the context from the start.

Graphic organizers are commonly used by teachers, and many course texts include graphic organizers as a means for illustrating and describing an idea or concept. While these can be greatly helpful, they can also be confusing when different ones are used to depict the same concept and when there is little consistency as to how often they are used. It is not uncommon, for example, for elementary school ELs and students with learning differences and learning disabilities to be instructed by more than one teacher. An EL may be taught by a grade-level classroom teacher, ESL teacher, bilingual teacher, and Title 1 teacher. Each of these teachers may choose a different graphic organizer to teach the same concept.

For example, think of the concept *same and different* and apply it to the following: *ways in which an elementary school and a middle school are the same and different.* One teacher may choose to use a Venn diagram to illustrate this idea (Figure 5.1), whereas another might use a different type of graphic organizer (Figure 5.2), and a third might choose to be creative and design an entirely different visual to illustrate the same concept.

Figure 5.1   Venn Diagram Showing How an Elementary School and a Middle School Are the Same and Different

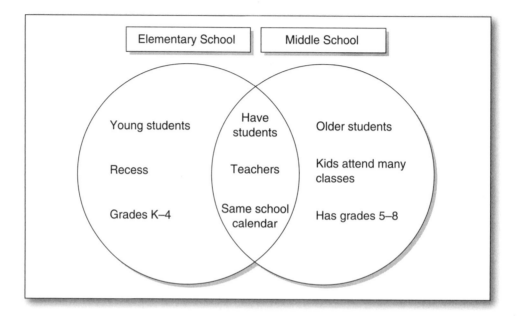

Figure 5.2   Another Visual Showing How an Elementary School and a Middle School Are the Same and Different

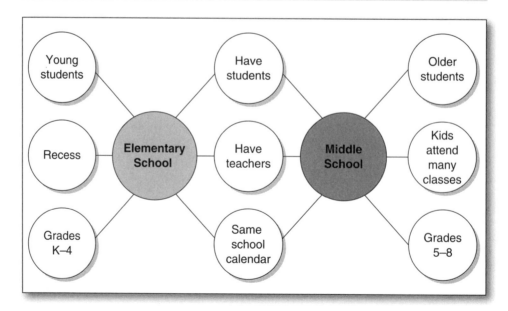

While the intent of a graphic organizer is to help to make concepts and ideas more meaningful, school leaders should help teachers select specific organizers that will be used to depict the various concepts, as the usage of more than one can create confusion rather than provide access to ELs. Let's look closely at the various reasons for selecting a graphic organizer:

We use visuals to organize our thoughts, connecting a concept relationship to an idea, in eight ways (Hyerle et al., 2004):

- brainstorming
- describing
- sequencing/ordering
- comparing/contrasting
- classifying/grouping
- whole-part relationships
- describing cause-effect relationships
- seeing analogies

While these eight elements are not directly the core curriculum that is taught, they are essential means for teaching the curriculum and, more important, helping students engage in a thinking process in order to learn. In a real sense, each time we use a graphic organizer, we help students visually map concepts. This can break down when there is no consistency among the type of organizers that are used. When the same organizer is used to teach any one of these important eight elements, it provides a good conceptual anchor for students, particularly ELs who are learning new content and language simultaneously and must rely on the familiar to make a connection with new information. In the earlier question that was posed, for example, one graphic organizer would have been much more helpful for understanding the compare/contrast concept. Graphic organizers of any sort must be explicitly taught to students. They cannot simply be written on the board. Gathering a team of elementary grade-level, secondary subject matter, resource, and specialist teachers can be a very helpful means for school and district leaders to develop the routine organizer that will be used for each concept.[1] Leaders can play an integral role to ensure that these important visuals are consistent and, therefore, more accessible for all learners.

Each of these eight principles should be used to effectively deliver a lesson. The checklist found in Resource 5.1 can help teachers and their supervisors assess the overall effectiveness of the planning and delivery of lessons. The next chapter will discuss the importance of engaging parents in their children's education.

---

[1] The trademarked term *Thinking Maps* was developed for describing the eight types of thinking processes that are used when engaging in a learning task.

RESOURCE 5.1
Checklist for Designing and Delivering Quality Learning Experiences

1. ☐ I have taken time to connect the academic learning experience to socially relevant issues that are personal to my students' lives in the following ways:

2. ☐ My lessons connect with my students' personal, cultural, language, and prior academic experiences.

3. ☐ I have designed pair and small-group tasks and activities that will engage my students in multiple opportunities to practice using and applying the language of content.

4. ☐ I have specifically taught my students how to engage in pair and group work.

5. ☐ I have designed activities that will help my students examine their group's process in pair and group work.

6. ☐ I have designed activities that will help my students examine their group's product in pair and group work.

7. ☐ I know the English proficiency levels of the ELs in my classroom and have planned activities and tasks that are targeted to these levels.

8. ☐ I have assigned roles that my ELs will do in pair and group settings that match their level of English proficiency.

9. ☐ I have provided my ELs with in-class practice of the tasks and assignments that they will do at home. I have also modified these to match each EL's current level of English proficiency.

10. ☐ I have taken time to phrase the overarching objectives of the unit in a meaningful way to help my students understand its purpose.

11. ☐ I have posted my daily lesson's content (i.e., learning) and language objectives (i.e., what students will do to learn) on the board in clear and simple language (and checked for student comprehension).

12. ☐ I have identified the important terms, words, idioms, and phrases (TWIPs) that my student needs to learn this subject matter and posted these on the board using categories and illustrations to make them meaningful.

13. ☐ I have identified the graphic organizers that I will use to display the concepts that I want my students to learn. These include organizers that will help my students brainstorm, describe, order, compare/contrast, classify, and/or display whole to part, cause-effect, or analogy relationships.

14. ☐ I have modeled the tasks and activities that my students will do and stated directions in simple language.

15. ☐ I have modeled and explicitly taught the thinking skills that my students will use.

REFERENCES

Anderson, L. W., & Krathwohl, D. R. (Eds.). (2001). *A taxonomy for learning, teaching and assessing: A revision of Bloom's Taxonomy of educational objectives: Complete edition.* New York: Longman.

August, D., & Shanahan, T. (2006). *Literacy in second language learners: Report of the National Literacy Panel on Language Minority Children and Youth.* Mahwah, NJ: Lawrence Erlbaum.

August, D., & Shanahan, T. (2008). *Developing reading and writing in second language learners: Lessons from a report of the National Literacy Panel on Language Minority Children and Youth.* New York: Routledge.

Bandura, A. (1977). *Social learning theory.* New York: General Learning Press.

Beck, I. L., McKeown, M. G., Kucan, L. (2002). *Bringing words to life: Robust vocabulary instruction.* New York: Guilford Press.

Blatner, W. (2006). *Final paper.* Unpublished manuscript, University of Massachusetts at Amherst.

Bloom, B. S., & Krathwohl, D. R. (1956). *Taxonomy of educational objectives: The classification of educational goals, by a committee of college and university examiners. Handbook 1: Cognitive domain.* New York: Longman.

Caine, R. N., & Caine, G. (1991). *Making connections: Teaching and the human brain.* Reading, MA: Addison-Wesley.

Caine, R. N., Caine, G., McClintic, C., & Klimek, K. (2005). *12 brain/mind learning principles in action: The fieldbook for making connections, teaching, and the human brain.* Thousand Oaks, CA: Corwin.

Calderón, M. (2007). Teaching reading to English language learners, grades 6–12: A framework for improving achievement in the content areas. Thousand Oaks, CA: Corwin.

Calderón, M. (2009, March). Expediting reading comprehension for English language learners. Presentation at the annual convention of Teachers of English to Speakers of Other Languages, Denver, CO.

Calderón, M. E., & Minaya-Rowe, L. (2010). *Preventing long-term ELs: transforming schools to meet core standards.* Thousand Oaks, CA: Corwin.

Cohen, E. G. (1994). *Designing groupwork: Strategies for the heterogeneous classroom* (2nd ed.). New York: Teachers College Press.

Collier, V. (1995). Acquiring a second language for school. *Directions in Language and Education, 1*(4). Retrieved December 18, 2010, from http://www.eric.ed .gov/ERICWebPortal/recordDetail?accno=ED394301

Echevarria, J., Vogt, M., & Short, D. (2002). *The SIOP model: Sheltered instruction for academic achievement.* Washington, DC: Center for Applied Linguistics.

Gardner, H. (2009). *Five minds for the future.* Cambridge, MA: Harvard University Press.

Gebhard, M. (2002/2003). Getting past "See Spot Run." *Educational Leadership, 60*(4), 35–39.

Genesee, F., Lindholm-Leary, K., Saunders, W., & Christian, D. (2006). *Educating English language learners.* New York: Cambridge University Press.

Goldenberg, C., & Coleman, R. (2010). *Promoting academic achievement among English learners: A guide to the research.* Thousand Oaks, CA: Corwin.

Haynes, J., & Zacarian, D. (2010). *Teaching English language learners across the content areas.* Alexandria, VA: Association for Supervision and Curriculum Development.

Hinkel, E. (2009, March). *Teaching academic vocabulary and helping students retain it.* Paper presented at the annual convention of Teachers of English to Speakers of Other Languages, Denver, CO.

Hubec, J., & Short, D. (Producers). (2002). *The SIOP model: Sheltered instruction for academic achievement* [Videotape]. Washington, DC: Author.

Hyerle, D., Curtis, S., & Alpert, L. (Eds.). (2004). *Student successes with Thinking Maps: School-based research, results, and models for achievement using visual tools.* Thousand Oaks, CA: Corwin.

Jensen, E. (2005). *Teaching with the brain in mind* (2nd ed.). Alexandria, VA: Association for Supervision and Curriculum Development.

Johnson, D. W., & Johnson, R. T. (1985). The internal dynamics of cooperative learning groups. In R. Slavin, S. Sharan, S. Kagan, R. H. Lazarowitz, C. Webb, & R. Schmuck (Eds.), *Learning to cooperate, cooperating to learn* (pp. 103–124). New York: Plenum Press.

Johnson, D. W., Johnson, R. T., & Johnson Holubec, E. (1986). *Circles of learning: Cooperation in the classroom* (Rev. ed.). Edina, MN: Interaction Book Company.

Krashen, S. D. (2002). Second language acquisition and second language learning. Retrieved December 21, 2010, from http://top-pdf.com/download/krashen-second-language-acquisition-download-2.html

Lee, G. (1991). *China boy.* New York: Random House.

Lee, G. (2000, May). *Keynote speech.* Presentation at the Annual MATSOL Conference, Leominster, MA.

Marzano, R. (2010, March). *Building academic background knowledge in English language learners.* Workshop presentation at the Annual Convention of Teachers of English to Speakers of Other Languages, Boston.

Marzano, R. J., & Pickering, D. J. (2005). *Building academic vocabulary: Teacher's manual.* Alexandria, VA: Association for Supervision and Curriculum Development.

Massachusetts Racial and Gender Profiling Technical Report. (2004). Boston: Northeastern University, Institute on Race and Justice. Retrieved December 21, 2010, from http://www.mass.gov/Eeops/docs/eops/Racial_and_Gender_Profiling_Study.pdf

Pransky, K. (2008). *Beneath the surface: The hidden realities of teaching culturally and linguistically diverse young learners, K–6.* Portsmouth, NH: Heinemann.

Pransky, K., & Zacarian, D. (2011). *Teacher's guide to providing rich vocabulary instruction.* Northampton, MA: Collaborative for Educational Services.

Sylwester, R., & Cho, J.-Y. (1992). What brain research says about paying attention. *Educational Leadership, 50*(4), 71–76.

Vasquez, V. (2010). *Getting beyond "I like the book": Creating space for critical literacy in K–6 classrooms* (2nd ed.). Newark, DE: International Reading Association.

Vatterott, C. (2009). *Rethinking homework: Best practices that support diverse needs.* Alexandria, VA: Association for Supervision and Curriculum Development.

Wiggins, G., & McTighe, J. (2005), *Understanding by design* (expanded 2nd ed.). Alexandria, VA: Association for Supervision and Curriculum Development.

Zacarian, D. (1996). Learning how to teach and design curriculum for the heterogeneous class: An ethnographic study of a task-based cooperative learning group of native English and English as a second language speakers in a graduate education course. *Dissertation Abstract International.* (UMI No. 963 9055)

6

Emphasizing the Importance of Parent Engagement

When Sokhem arrived to take the SAT, he was 15 minutes late.[1] The public transportation that he normally took to school during the week ran on a different schedule on the weekend. When he arrived at 8:15, the monitor would not let him in. She told Sokhem that the testing had begun at 8:00 and the door was closed. He almost broke down in tears as she shut the door, refusing him entry. He returned to the bus stop and waited for over an hour for the bus to return him to his house. When he finally arrived home and told his mother what happened, he cried, "Now, I will never go to college!"

Sokhem's mother was not sure what to do. She knew that his school was having an Open House for parents soon. Thinking that would be a good time to ask his teachers for help, she took time off from work to help her son—though she would miss a much-needed day of pay. On Open House night, she waited anxiously in a line that was marked for parents of 11th graders whose last name began with the letters A–G. When she reached the sign-in table, she tried to muster the courage to seek help for her son. But before she could, she was shuttled off to Sokhem's first-period math class. She politely waited while the math teacher described the math course to all of the parents so she could speak with him about Sokhem.

---

[1]This example is drawn from Zacarian (2007a).

However, the teacher spoke so quickly that she could not keep up with him. Suddenly, at the end of 10 minutes, a bell rang and the school principal announced over the loudspeaker that parents should go to their child's next class. Sokhem's mother reluctantly got up from her seat and tried to capture the math teacher's attention. However, all he did was reach for the course schedule that she was holding and tell her where to go for Sokhem's second-period class. This same scenario continued throughout the Open House event. Sokhem's mother went from class to class hoping that she could get advice from one of his teachers. By the last class, she was exhausted. She had been rushed from one classroom to the next, one side of the building to the other, and had not been able to ask her important question. She was not empowered enough to stop the flow of the Open House night like a more empowered parent from the dominant culture would have been, nor did she have enough English language skill to do so.

When the bell rang for the last time, the school principal thanked everyone for coming, announced that the Open House was over, and bid everyone goodnight. So that she wouldn't be leaving without hearing anything to help her son, Sokhem's mother mustered the courage to speak to his last-period instructor, who happened to be his ESL teacher. The ESL teacher, though anxious to go home, took time to talk with her about Sokhem's problem. The teacher helped her understand that she and her son needn't worry, that there would be other opportunities to take the SAT. The next day, the ESL teacher found Sokhem and helped him make plans to take the SAT the next time the test was offered in the area.

The following year, when Sokhem had scored well on the SAT, graduated high school, and was excitedly getting ready to attend a local college, he told his ESL teacher that he could not have done it without her and his mother's help. She began to reflect on the experience that she had had with Sokhem's mother. Could she and the school have been more proactive to help students and their parents with the college application process?

THE IMPORTANCE OF FAMILY ENGAGEMENT

The importance of family-school engagement is well documented (Delpit, 1995; Espinosa, 2010; Henderson, Mapp, Johnson, & Davies, 2007; Lawrence-Lightfoot, 1999, 2003). Establishing relationships with parents and extended families should be an important objective for school leaders at all grade levels. Superintendents, principals, curriculum directors, and all leaders should make this an important priority. While much has been written about parent partnerships at the early childhood level (Ballantyne, Sanderman, & McLaughlin, 2008; Espinosa, 2010; Tabors, 1998), maintaining strong partnerships with the families of English learners (ELs) should continue through high school. We may be familiar with the importance of parent involvement, but we sometimes overlook its special relevance for parents from linguistically and culturally diverse backgrounds.

Many teachers and administrators are not familiar with the various cultural norms of ELs and their families. Conversely, many parents of ELs are not familiar with the culture of the American public school, in terms of its implied ways of thinking, being, and acting. These are implied by the dominant culture's notion of "school culture."[2] Misconceptions and misunderstandings abound on both sides, and these differences can easily become impenetrable barriers that divide and separate one group from another. Differences can also be exacerbated by the realities of (1) a largely untrained educational community in such important areas as second language acquisition, multicultural education, and methods for working with ELs and their families and (2) families who are not familiar with American public school practices (Haynes & Zacarian, 2010).

Moreover, parents, teachers, and administrators may hold a variety of misconceptions about what it takes to educate second language learners well. For example, they may think that using more than one language is a problem instead of a resource (Espinosa, 2010; Stechuk, Burns, & Yandian, 2006). Students' best interests can be lost in a sea of misinformation and misassumptions about language learning as well as the cultural divide (Zacarian, 2006, 2007a, 2008b).

The Open House example from the beginning of the chapter is a common one in public schools across the United States. Of course, many parents do understand the norms and expectations of this event—because it is a very familiar facet of our culture and has existed for generations (Lawrence-Lightfoot, 2003). For example, most parents of secondary students know that they will be standing in line for their child's schedule at the Open House night. And if they don't know what is going on, they can freely ask a peer for help. Let's look at the following exchange between an American monolingual English-speaking parent of a freshman and a peer who has a freshman and an older child attending the high school.

Parent 1:   So what do we do now?

Parent 2:   You'll get Janet's Monday class schedule. The bell'll ring, you'll hear Mr. Martin [the school principal] announce that we'll go to our kids' first-period class. It'll last about 10 minutes. Bell'll ring again and we'll go to our kids' second class. If Janet has a study hall, you can go to the cafeteria for cookies and coffee and to learn about the Parent Council. Definitely stop there, the cookies are usually good!

---

[2]In this book, the terms *culture* and *cultural way of being* are used to refer to two groups: (a) ELs and their families who are from diverse cultural experiences other than the dominant monolingual American English-speaking culture and (b) monolingual American English-speaking students, educators, parents, and community members. Drawing from Trueba, Guthrie, and Au (1981), these terms are used to describe "a form of communication with learned and shared, explicit and implicit rules for perceiving, believing, evaluating, and acting. . . . What people talk about and are specific about, such as traditional customs and laws, constitutes their overt or explicit culture. What they take for granted, or what exists beyond conscious awareness, is their implicit culture" (pp. 4–5).

In this short exchange, the first parent learns that he will attend an abbreviated school day and listen to a quick overview of his child's classes, and that there are good snacks as well as information about the parent council in the cafeteria. It's likely that this parent already knew that an Open House is not a time to ask questions about one's own child, as he has been to all of his child's Open Houses since kindergarten. He has been "trained" to ask questions about his child during another routine cultural event: parent conferences. It's also likely that he has attended parent conferences since his child was in kindergarten. Thus, in the above exchange, a lot of implied rules have already been learned, and it is likely that the inquiring parent quickly understands the rules and can follow them easily because he has so much applicable background experience. In this sense, he is well positioned to adapt to the new context and participate meaningfully in it.

The same cannot be said of parents of ELs. School events are unfamiliar to many parents of ELs and can even seem unwelcoming at times. In addition, these parents do not often have access to the same peer resources as parents from the dominant group have.

It is typical for parents to learn about school practices from peers who are like themselves. As in all human societies, we tend to associate with others like ourselves. We feel more comfortable and safe with, and ask questions of, others from our own group when possible; this is particularly true among minority groups (Allport, 1979; Tatum, 1997). So naturally, it is typical for parents to learn about school practices from peers who are like them. This reality is highly relevant for school leaders to consider for two reasons. First, American public school practices reflect dominant culture norms, which include a host of implied rules for acting and being. Most parents of ELs are not so familiar with American dominant culture norms, thus they are not very familiar with the hidden rules of American public schools and are likely to be uncomfortable asking for help from others outside of their own cultural group. Second, unless schools create safe places in which the implied rules are explained explicitly until they are well understood, parents may feel and be disconnected from their child's school.

Indeed, almost all school events and activities, including parent conferences, potluck suppers, football games, field trips, driver's education, school plays, and signing up for basketball and soccer, are cultural activities. Successful interaction involves knowing the appropriate rules for engaging in these activities as well as what is and is not expected. Routine events that are emblematic of a school are familiar and welcoming for English-fluent American families and anyone else who knows the event's predictable routines, practices, and outcomes. However, these events pose unique challenges for parents and teachers of ELs alike when neither is familiar with the other's cultural expectations and rules.

It should be clear by now that school leaders must create and implement new routines and practices that take into account the unique needs of their EL parent population, to ensure that all are welcomed and can become active members of the school community. In the example at the beginning of the chapter, Sokhem and his mother were at a clear disadvantage. They did not know the rules for taking the SAT and were entirely reliant on Sokhem's school to make this knowledge explicit. At the same time, it was only luck that connected Sokhem's mother with his empathetic ESL teacher. Schools should be proactive about creating meaningful connections to families, not reactive or leaving it to luck. In a certain sense, commonly occurring events such as the one in this example puts ELs, their families, and others in a lower-status position than that of the dominant group because they lack familiarity with and knowledge about those common practices. This lack of familiarity can also perpetuate the status quo of being in a powerless position. Ideally, school leaders must create spaces that are built on mutual respect and ensure the allocation of equal status for all. This requires school leaders to think *carefully, empathetically, and proactively* about the ways in which parents can become active members and partners in their child's education.

CREATING MEANINGFUL PARTNERSHIPS WITH PARENTS

All families should be considered as rich resources, as people who have something important to contribute. School leaders need to set the right tone for this to be possible. This requires school leaders to pay close attention to what Henderson et al. (2007) aptly name *partnership schools*, which require school leaders to have a deep belief in, and commitment to, the notion that parents are important contributors to ensuring the success of all students. *Contribution,* in a broad sense, refers to having a high level of respect for, deep appreciation of, and interest in cultural differences as rich and valuable assets with which to build partnerships. Drawing from Henderson et al., Espinosa (2010), Delpit, (1995), and Zacarian (2007b, 2008a, 2008b), four elements form the framework for creating strong parent-school partnerships. The four elements cannot be accomplished in isolation; each is dependent on the other.

Framework for parent–school partner schools

1. **Bridging the cultural divide**
   - Make routines and practices transparent, meaningful, and accessible for parents of ELs.
   - Create events and activities that pay particular attention to families of ELs and their cultural ways of being.
   - Encourage parent involvement throughout all grade levels in a manner that is respectful of parents.

2. **Infusing parent advocacy as part of the core**
   - Help parents become a powerful influence in their child's education.
   - Understand the EL community and its needs to support EL parent advocacy.

3. **Linking parent involvement to learning**
   - Connect parent and family activities with learning.
   - Connect learning to what is happening at home and in the community.

4. **Working together for the common good of students**
   - School leaders and parents work together to create a welcoming climate.
   - School leaders and parents work with the community to improve student outcomes and their connections with the community.

The following example illustrates this framework.

When a group of elementary-aged students from El Salvador and Puerto Rico enrolled in Crocker Farm School, in Amherst, Massachusetts, they and their families were unable to communicate in English. In addition, some of the students had only limited documents about their prior schooling. A bilingual translator conducted an interview with all of the parents to learn as much possible about the children's and their parents' prior schooling experiences (see Chapter 3, Resource 3.5 for a sample of suggested interview questions). The interview was conducted in Spanish to allow for a free flow of comfortable conversation. During the interview, it was learned that some of the children had had limited prior schooling. They had attended school for just a few hours a day and were unable to attend on a regular basis. Their parents had also had limited prior schooling.

While all of the parents wanted their child to do well in school, they didn't know much about their child's prior educational programming. In addition, the translator learned that it would have been inappropriate for parents to be involved in their child's schooling in their native countries. Their cultural beliefs were that teachers and the school were the all-knowing authority and that it was not parents' place to question teachers about their child's educational programming. However, the translator also knew that it was appropriate for parents to be involved in any social programming and events, as this was a commonly held practice in her own culture, and she knew to ask about it during the parent interviews.

Based in large part on these parent interviews, Crocker Farm School leaders saw three challenges. First, they needed to create a program that would benefit students with interrupted schooling. Second, they wanted to create a program in which Latino students would not be isolated from their American monolingual English-speaking peers. Third, to build community, they knew that they needed to honor and build on the assets of the parent community.

To build community and honor parents as assets, they decided to organize a play that students would perform entirely in Spanish. With the complete support of the school principal, a small group of mixed monolingual English and bilingual Spanish/English staff held tryouts for the play. The teachers distributed bilingual Spanish/English flyers to the school community about the play and the tryouts. They held an art contest for the advertising that would be included in the playbill. The tryouts occurred after school and finished in time for students to catch the "late" bus. The play had 20 speaking parts, but over 50 Spanish- and English-speaking students came to the tryouts! In response, the teachers decided to expand the play to include singing, dancing, and acting parts so that everyone could be selected and have an important role in the play. English- and Spanish-speaking students learned Latin ballroom dancing, a Spanish song, and dialogue in Spanish. During the initial interviews, the outreach worker learned that one of the parents of an EL was a seamstress. When she shared this with the staff, they reached out to the parent for help in creating and sewing the costumes. She happily agreed and solicited further support from additional parents of ELs and community members. Other parents of ELs and local businesspeople from the town's Latino restaurants were recruited to help in additional ways, including providing the snacks that would be served during the play's conclusion. Within a short period of time, parents and community members who had never before been involved in their child's schooling gladly volunteered to help. The school bustled with activities related to the play, and there was a steady stream of English-fluent and non-English-speaking parents working side by side helping with the play's preparation.

On opening night, the auditorium was filled to capacity. Knowing that many of the parents of ELs worked morning, afternoon, and sometimes evening shifts, several performances were held, before, during, and after school. Each was well attended and, more often than not, at standing room only capacity. Quickly, word about the wonderful play spread through the town, and within a few days two of the town's other schools asked if the students could perform the play in their school. By the play's end, the number of parent volunteers swelled to the highest in the school's history, as did the play's attendance. In addition, some of the newcomer Spanish-speaking students became renowned in the school and, more important, their parents became more comfortable in their child's school. There were many other successes worth noting, the following two in particular: Students and parents from both cultures engaged more actively with each other, and monolingual English-speaking students learned Spanish. So what did the school do that worked so well?

Bridging the cultural divide

Family outreach is critical. Whether schools have high or low incidences of ELs, partnerships can be built only when parents have working knowledge about a school's routines and practices, *and* when school leaders, teachers, and other staff have a working knowledge of students' and parents' culture and language. Bilingual outreach workers, whether volunteer parents, teachers, counselors, or others, are essential for building this important knowledge. Outreach workers need the following skills:

- strong communication skills in both English and the parents' home language
- insider knowledge about the school system and how it works
- a high level of trust within the parent community

It is important to be as proactive as possible with bilingual outreach. It should begin at enrollment as doing so makes it much more likely that parents will feel welcomed. As seen in Chapter 1, some parents of ELs have prior educational experiences that are similar to or matched with their child's, whereas others do not. Schools need to be culturally sensitive to ensure that diverse communities of parents are fully integrated in the school community. Outreach is an important element for building community. The value of outreach is twofold:

- It helps parents understand the routines and practices of school.
- It helps the school understand the parent community.

When a school has identified ELs, it is important to then proactively provide outreach. Some schools have trained bilingual bicultural outreach workers on their staff. Generally, these professionals have advanced knowledge and skills in counseling, community service, or a related field and are members of the culture and language group of a school's dominant EL population. Other schools solicit help from parent volunteers, support staff, teachers, guidance counselors, and other educators to perform this important role. It is essential that it be performed by a parent community "insider" who also has depth of knowledge about how a school works and its educational programming. When the school employs people who have this dual identity—deeply connected to the parents' culture on the one hand, and fully integrated into the school's preferred ways of being and acting on the other—it is very fortunate to get a direct pipeline to an "outsider" perspective on their school, which otherwise it might never see. This includes both the implicit as well as the school's more obvious and explicit ways of being and acting.

Being able to take an outsider's point of view allows school leaders to look at the whole of what occurs during the school year and establish a means for explaining this explicitly to parents. In the example at the beginning of the chapter, for example, Sokhem and his mother would have been better informed had the school been able to take an outsider's view about the college application process. This would have happened had an outreach worker established a positive relationship with the parent, and her and her son's need for information about the college application process surfaced.

For example, the school enrollment process involves parents filling out a wide range of documents and receiving a lot of varied information about the school. The purpose of asking for much of what is gathered from parents is only implied. The school emergency card, for example, is a frequently used form that enables the school to contact parents or their designee in the event of an emergency. Some parents of ELs may not be familiar with what constitutes an emergency, and the words *emergency* and *designee* may be misconstrued. A bilingual bicultural outreach worker would be trained to explicitly explain the purpose of this important document and to respond to questions about it.

OUTREACH AS AN ESSENTIAL ENROLLMENT COMPONENT

Outreach workers should:

1. Assist parents with the registration process by explaining the following to students and their parents/guardians:

   Student's class schedule

   School schedule

   Extracurricular activities available to all students

   Lunch procedure and an explanation of the process by which students may participate in free and reduced lunch

   Student's right to equal access to an education

   Emergency card purpose and form

   Student handbook and code of conduct

2. Establish a routine means of communication to do the following:

   Address concerns that parents have

   Ensure that parents are routinely apprised of their child's academic progress

   Notify parents about important school-related information or extracurricular activities that were not communicated at enrollment

   Encourage parents to be active members of the school community

   Support parents to identify postgraduate plans that routinely occur for all students

   Familiarize parents with school-related activities and procedures

---

It is better to have ongoing outreach programs over the course of a school year than to have just one orientation meeting. A second important element for bridging the cultural divide is to create activities that pay particular attention to families of ELs and their cultural ways of being. The arts, including plays, music, dance, and other performance modes, are wonderful resources for involving parents. They are fun, engaging, and rouse parents' interest in participating in their child's schooling (Henderson et al., 2007).

In the second example, the bilingual bicultural counselor noted that one of the parents of an EL was a seamstress, and she shared this information with the group that organized the school play. The teachers reached out to this parent, and she eagerly helped create the costumes. She also solicited the help of other parents and community members in this effort. They became more familiar and comfortable with the school and its staff and students through the costume-making activity. This is an example of an asset-based model. To launch this type of model requires school leaders to set the tone for involving parents actively and comfortably in their child's school and involving their child as well. In the school play example, the event was delivered entirely in Spanish. The language used promoted the assets of the minority group. It allowed native speakers of Spanish to be powerful mentors of English-speaking peers and the dominant community to enjoy the benefits of a performance, albeit in a language with which they were not familiar. The principal's intentional leadership throughout this process greatly helped to bridge the cultural divide. This type of leadership and advocacy was also encouraged by the district's leaders, especially the superintendent, as part of its commitment to involving parents in their child's education.

Infusing parent advocacy as part of the core

A child's biggest advocate is his or her parents. They know their child very well and want the best for him or her. However, schools are complex institutions that are difficult for even the most seasoned parent to navigate well, let alone parents of ELs. Leaders must be proactive in empowering and supporting parents of ELs to advocate for their child. One way of doing this is for school leaders to be fully committed to helping parents be comfortably and meaningfully integrated into the school community. The more contact that a school has with families in a positive way, the more opportunities for advocacy occur.

However, the typical belief among educators is that the parents who are involved in their child's schooling care about their child and those who are not involved according to dominant culture expectations do not (Finders & Lewis, 1994; Henderson et al., 2007). This is a deficit-based model in which particular groups of parents are perceived as not caring for their child. Parent involvement in their child's schooling is a type of advocacy. The more opportunities that parents have to be involved in ways in which they are comfortable, the more they can advocate for their child. Active and continuous involvement helps parents gain an insider's view through repeated exposure to the culture and practices of American public schools.

An asset-based partner model is one in which the school provides explicit knowledge to parents about their child's schooling so that parents can gain the knowledge that they need to do what they do best: advocate for their own child. Unless parents are given multiple and continuous opportunities to engage in this advocacy role, schools may find it challenging to regard parents as legitimate and valued partners in their child's education.

Advocacy should have a broad meaning so that it includes whatever is needed to help a student be committed to learning and doing well in school and a parent invested in helping the child to do so. A very important distinction must be made about the different perceptions that some groups have about time. North America and much of Europe place a high value on efficiency, structure, and organization concerning time (Hayes & Zacarian, 2010). American public schools represent this type of monochronic perception of time. Deadlines and schedules are important, participants do one thing at a time, promptness is valued, and school is tightly organized according to fixed time parameters. Conversely, Latin America, the Middle East, the Caribbean, Southern Europe, and Africa are not monochronic. Rather, time is perceived as flowing and as having no particular structure or predictability. Tardiness is not a problem. Personal relationships are of much higher value than is the management of time. Indeed, time is not seen as important to manage. This perception of time as polychronic is quite distinct from monochromic groups (Haynes & Zacarian, 2010).

When put into context, think of a school system that holds parent conferences and sends home to parents a note about the date and time of the conference. The institution of school runs along the ticking of the clock to keep the order of the conferences moving. The management of time is seen as crucial for this event and a priority. When parents do not respond to the parent conference invitation by either replying that they will or will not attend or not showing up on time, schools view this as an act of not caring. In reality, it is more likely a representation of a differing view about time. Another common example is the student who does not attend school for several days. For example, when a school learns that a student missed school because the student and his or her family traveled to visit other family members, the school perceives this behavior to mean that the student's parents do not care about their child's education. It is critical that schools pay attention to differing views about time without making evaluative judgments. While this is easier said than done, being aware of views about time can help schools address the challenges that occur as a result. Again, increasing the amount of opportunities that parents have to become familiar with school practices will help bridge these differences and promote the concept of parents as advocates.

Taking an outsider's view here is important, once again. Knowing that personal relationships are important for building partnerships with parents from polychronic cultures, it is important to create socializing activities at the beginning of the school year that give parents the opportunity to get to know their child's educators in a more personal way and to continue offering social activities throughout the school year. School leaders should carefully consider all of the events that typically occur during the school year that relate to the academic side of students' education, such as parent conferences, report card periods, and Open House, and precede these with activities that provide a more personal and social means for getting to know the families of ELs. Some schools do this through home visits, potluck suppers, and multicultural activities such as a family evening for Latin dancing. This approach to building personal relationships with parents parallels the cultural frame in which parents are familiar and comfortable.

ACTIVITIES TARGETED FOR BUILDING RELATIONSHIPS WITH FAMILIES

September 5: **Family picnic**—Parents, children, and staff are invited to bring a picnic dinner or snack and enjoy it on the school grounds. Cookies and fruit punch are furnished by the school. Bilingual bicultural staff/volunteers contact families about the event, support transportation plans to and from the event, and attend the event to ensure as smooth a picnic activity as possible.

September 15: **Multicultural potluck supper**—Parents, children, and staff gather for a potluck supper, bringing various dishes to share. Bilingual bicultural staff/volunteers contact families about the event and attend it to ensure as smooth an activity as possible. Music from the various communities of ELs is also shared.

October 1: **Open House**—Parents of ELs are invited an hour before the general parent population to learn about the evening's events. Bilingual bicultural staff/volunteers contact families and attend the Open House to ensure its success.

Linking parent involvement to learning

More often than not, we worry that parents who are not fluent in English cannot connect or support their child's education. We worry more with parents who are not literate in their native language or English in terms of their having the capacity to read academic text and help their child understand it. We may think this because we believe that learning is entirely academic. An alternate view is important here. Learning involves building connections between what students already know and what is unknown (Jensen, 1998). Using a brain-based model, the brain is a connection maker in that it takes what is known and connects it with what is not known. Learning occurs when these connections are made, but not all connections occur through academic experiences. They occur via students' personal, cultural, language, and world experiences as well (Haynes & Zacarian, 2010). Rousing students' interest to learn must include making connections with their personal, cultural, language, and world knowledge. Indeed, these connectors may be far more successful than drawing strictly from academic knowledge. Parents have a good deal to contribute in terms of their child's intellectual development. When parents are empowered, their knowledge can be used in powerful ways (Moll, 1992). For example, when a school principal noted that many of the fathers of the school's ELs were fishermen, he encouraged the ELs' teachers to develop a unit of study on the fishing industry. With help from the fathers and other members of the fishing community, various teachers designed and delivered successful interdisciplinary science, social studies, and language arts lessons on this topic.

While this is a helpful means for connecting to parents, much of academic text is built on implied understandings about American society. Think of the social studies teacher who asks the important question, "What is the relevance of Barack Obama being the first African American president?" This question requires depth of knowledge about race in America that many ELs do not possess. Helping to build connections to learning through students' and their families' prior experiences can be more easily accomplished if we consider the relevance of the other connection makers and include parents in the process. Drawing from Moll (1992), we must encourage educators to view the means by which parents' knowledge will be encouraged and empowered. In this sense, learning occurs when it is connected to what is happening at home and in the community. It is personal and cultural and built upon students' and their families' view of the world. For example, asking students to interview their parents about a time in which they were not treated well and/or were discriminated against can activate students' interest to study the relevance of the first African American president.

This asset-based model of connecting curriculum to ELs' personal, cultural, language, and world experiences provides opportunities for parents to help in their child's schooling by using the rich resources that they posses. When schools build systematic connections to students and their families' lives, there is a much greater chance that academic learning will occur.

Working together for the common good of students

Schools do not exist in a vacuum. They reside within communities in which students travel from one side of a city or town to their school, walk to school, or both. Creating a welcoming environment for an EL community and its culture requires a high level of commitment within the student and parent community as well as the community at large, and it requires more than celebrating cultural holidays and events. In the second example described earlier, the school involved community members in the production of a play. Local restaurant workers, seamstresses, and other community members became involved with the performance for the common good of the children, and their collective contributions are what made the performance successful. This type of effort requires a much broader lens. It involves a willingness on the part of the school, as well as the community, to look closely at itself.

It means taking time to learn about how the school's ELs are or are not participating in events and activities that are common among the dominant group. Town or city sports and driver's education programs, Girl and Boy Scouts and Boys and Girls Clubs, though generally not part of a school program, are often activities and groups that students engage in and that are part of their development. Because these are so common, teachers may draw from them to build connections to the curriculum. Think of a classroom teacher who uses a soccer example to illustrate a math problem. ELs and others may not be exposed to activities like playing on a soccer team because their parents cannot afford them and/or are not comfortable with them. Building partnerships with parents involves opening the circle of opportunity and involving all leaders in making this an important and sustained priority.

Parents of ELs can be more engaged in their child's education and school community when each of four frames are employed intentionally by school leaders—bridging the cultural divide, infusing parent advocacy as part of the core, linking parent involvement to learning, and working together for the common good of students. In the next chapter, we will explore ways to identify and work with ELs with learning differences and learning disabilities.

REFERENCES

Allport, D. (1979). *The nature of prejudice: The classic study of the roots of discrimination* (25th anniv. ed.). New York: Basic Books.

Ballantyne, K. B., Sanderman, A. R., McLaughlin, N. (2008). *Dual language learners in the early years: Getting ready to succeed in school.* Washington, DC: National Clearinghouse for English Language Acquisition. Retrieved December 22, 2010, from http://www.ncela.gwu.edu/files/uploads/3/DLLs_in_the_Early_Years.pdf

Delpit, L. (1995). *Other people's children: Cultural conflict in the classroom.* New York: New Press.

Espinosa, L. (2010). *Getting it right for young children from diverse backgrounds: Applying research to improve practice.* Upper Saddle River, NJ: Pearson.

Finders, M., & Lewis, C. (1994). Why some parents don't come to school. *Educating for Diversity, 51*(8), 50–54.

Haynes, J., & Zacarian, D. (2010). *Teaching English language learners across the content areas.* Alexandria, VA: Association for Supervision and Curriculum Development.

Henderson, A. T., Mapp, K. L. Johnson, V. R., & Davies, D. (2007). *Beyond the bake sale: The essential guide to family-school partnerships.* New York: New Press.

Jensen, E. (1998). *Teaching with the brain in mind.* Alexandria, VA: Association for Supervision and Curriculum Development.

Lawrence-Lightfoot, S. (1999). *Respect: An exploration.* Reading, MA: Perseus Books.

Lawrence-Lightfoot, S. (2003). The essential conversation: What parents and teachers can learn from each other. New York: Random House.

Moll, L. (1992). Bilingual classroom studies and community analysis: Some recent trends. *Educational Researcher, 21,* 20–24.

Stechuk, R. A., Burns, M. S., Yandian, S. E. (2006). *Bilingual infant/toddler environments: Supporting language and learning in our youngest children: A guide for migrant and seasonal head start programs.* Washington, DC: Academy for Educational Development. Retrieved December 23, 2010, from http://www.aed .org/Publications/upload/BITE_web1106.pdf

Tabors, P. O. (1998, November). What early childhood educators need to know: Developing effective programs for linguistically diverse children and families. *Young Children,* pp. 20–26. Retrieved December 22, 2010, from http:// www.naeyc.org/files/tyc/file/WhatECENeedToKnow.pdf

Tatum, B. D. (1997). *"Why are all of the Black kids sitting together in the cafeteria?" And other conversations about race.* New York: Basic Books.

Trueba, H., Guthrie, G. P., & Au, K. H. (1981). *Culture and the classroom: Studies in classroom ethnography.* Rowley, MA: Newbury House.

Zacarian, D. (2006). The [im]possibilities of social services. *Essential Teacher, 3*(3), 10–11.

Zacarian, D. (2007a). I can't go to college! *Essential Teacher, 4*(4), 10–11.

Zacarian, D. (2007b). Mascot or member? 4(3), 10–11.

Zacarian, D. (2008a). Finding the right interpreter is harder than you might think. *Essential Teacher, 5*(2), 10–11.

Zacarian, D. (2008b). Joinfostering the missing. *Essential Teacher, 5*(3), 10–11.

a disability. This traditionally included the application of the Wechsler Intelligence Scale for Children (WISC-IV) and an evaluation of student performance in class, on report cards, and on other standardized tests. Proponents of the reauthorization argued that these tests were often biased against students from diverse cultural and linguistic communities and resulted in the misdiagnosis and labeling of students with disabilities (Artiles, Trent, & Palmer, 2004; Donovan & Cross, 2002; Klingner & Edwards, 2007). The most recent reauthorization of IDEA allows schools to provide interventions *before* a student is referred for a special education evaluation. The purpose of these early interventions is to better ensure that students receive the supports that they need when they are needed so that fewer students will be referred and misdiagnosed as having a disability, especially students from culturally and linguistically diverse backgrounds.

Let's look at two scenarios of the same student, Li, a five-year-old kindergartener, to illustrate the types of interventions that are now allowed under IDEA. As you read the first scenario, ask yourself if you think that Li has a disability or whether the problem is socially constructed. If it is the latter, what might the school have done to more effectively provide for Li's instructional needs? As you read the second scenario, pay close attention to the steps that Li's teacher takes to provide interventions that she and others think will be helpful. We begin with a short description of Li, which is followed by a description of the two different responses that the school took to address her behavior.

Li was born in a rural province outside of Beijing. Shortly after she was born, her parents moved to the United States to complete their graduate studies and left Li in China, entrusting her to the care of her paternal grandparents. During her first five years, Li spoke solely in Mandarin, her grandparents were her sole caretakers, and she did not attend preschool. In August of her fifth year, her grandparents lovingly put Li on a plane bound for the United States, where she was reunited with her parents. Her parents' plan was for Li to begin attending kindergarten in the local public school a few weeks after her arrival. Thinking that it was important for Li to begin speaking in English, her parents decided that it was important for them to communicate with her solely in English.

When Li arrived in the United States, she was unable to understand her parents or the English-speaking environment in which they lived. In frustration, she spent her first few weeks crying, having temper tantrums, and begging that she could return to her grandparents. When Li began attending kindergarten, she was placed in an English-only classroom where she was the sole Mandarin speaker. Because of limited time and scheduling conflicts, Li's school allotted one 20-minute block of time per week for Li to receive ESL classes. The school justified this action based on the belief that kindergarten classes included a language-rich environment where ELs would flourish and that five-year-olds learned English quickly and without much help.

During Li's first month in school, she rarely interacted with her peers, and when she did, it was usually to grab something from them. Her teacher frequently observed Li kicking other students and being unable to perform most of the tasks that were assigned. At the end of Li's first month in school, her teacher held a parent conference to express the concerns that she had about Li's poor academic progress and inappropriate behavior. At the meeting, Li's parents told the teacher that Li was a "difficult" child.

Example 1: Thinking that a referral might be helpful, the teacher suggested that Li be referred to see whether she had a special education need. Her parents agreed with the teacher, thinking that the school knew what was best for their child. During the ensuing weeks, Li was tested in English by the school psychologist, speech and language therapist, and special educator to determine whether she had a disability. By the end of her first term in kindergarten, Li was diagnosed as having significant emotional and cognitive disabilities. In addition to her kindergarten teacher, she began working with a speech and language therapist, the school counselor, and a special educator in an all-English learning environment. She rarely attended her kindergarten class with her peers. Rather, the specialists with whom she worked took Li out of class, where she received a variety of supports that they believed were targeted for addressing her disabilities. When her teachers met with Li's parents at the end of the school year, they recommended that Li repeat kindergarten. Her parents agreed with this plan.

Example 2: Li's teacher asked the school counselor, psychologist, speech and language therapist, and special educator to join her in meeting with Li's parents. Wanting more information about Li, the group asked her parents to describe what she had been like as a younger child. When they learned that Li had lived with her paternal grandparents in China and had not lived with her parents until just prior to enrolling in kindergarten, they asked if Li had heard or spoken English prior to arriving in the United States. They also asked Li's parents if she had attended preschool. The teachers and specialists learned that Li spoke only in Mandarin, had not attended preschool, and had not had much contact with her parents during her first five years of life. A much clearer picture of Li emerged as a result of the meeting. Several prereferral interventions were recommended, including that Li speak in Mandarin at home and that her parents meet with the school counselor to discuss various parenting strategies. In addition, a Chinese interpreter was employed to work in Li's kindergarten class to help Li understand her kindergarten environment and to support her in communicating with her teacher and peers. The school psychologist and counselor often visited with Li while during her lunch and helped her engage more appropriately with her peers. Li also received a more appropriate amount of instruction in English language development: an hour per day from an ESL teacher. The kindergarten and ESL teachers collaborated closely and often codelivered lessons that they thought would benefit Li and her classmates. For example, during a unit about what makes a family, Li and her peers were encouraged to bring in family photos, draw pictures of their home, and use these visuals to talk about their family. Li brought in several photos of her grandparents and parents and drew some beautiful pictures of her home in China and in the United States. She readily shared these with her peers and began to converse in English more fluently. By the close of her kindergarten year, Li was able to communicate in English, was working well with her peers, and was making remarkable progress. Her parents and teachers were delighted with her accomplishments, and plans were made for her to attend the first grade.

The two scenarios about the same student provide us with very helpful information about what is allowed under IDEA as well as the types of interventions that are important to consider. In the first scenario, Li's teacher observed her behavior and performance in class and decided to refer her for a special education evaluation for two reasons: inappropriate behavior and poor school performance. When Li's parents commented that she was a "difficult" child, it confirmed the kindergarten teacher's assumptions that Li had behavioral issues. Li was also tested solely in English despite the reality that she had not yet had the opportunity to learn English and was not able to do ordinary class work in English. It is likely that she was tested using a discrepant model whereby her performance on tests (such as the WISC-IV) was used to compare how well she did in comparison with particular test norms. As stated earlier, the process of misidentifying and making assumptions about ELs is an altogether common dilemma and has led to national concern about the high incidence of overidentifying ELs as having disabilities. The first scenario provides an example of misidentifying an EL as having a disability as well as a rush to judgment.

The second scenario shows us the steps that can be taken to help a student such as Li be successful in school.

Providing sound general education programming before referring students for a special education evaluation

In the second scenario, Li's school took time to examine the effectiveness of its programming. It found that it was not providing ELs in kindergarten with enough ESL instructional time. It increased Li's ESL class time from 30 minutes per week to an hour per day. Also, it was seen that Li could not grasp the instructional program because it was delivered solely in English. A bilingual Mandarin/English-speaking translator was employed to help Li meaningfully understand the instruction and communicate with her peers and teacher. The school did this because it needed to look more closely at the type of programming that has been found to be the most successful, as described in Chapter 2, and its application of this proven-effective model.

Various specialists intervened immediately in the general classroom setting to help Li behave more appropriately with her peers and to learn. The examples of the interventions that were employed reflect the types of activities that are allowed under IDEA. The intent of interventions is to prevent students from being overidentified as having disabilities by immediately providing supports that will help them be successful in school. With Li, the school provided a tiered RTI model. Each of the interventions occurred in her general education classes and did not require her to be referred for special education or diagnosed with a disability.

WHAT IS RTI?

RTI is a means by which school systems systematically provide interventions when they are needed to prevent students from failing. The intent of an RTI model is to offer levels of interventions for addressing student failure as it is occurring and without waiting for a special education evaluation (Hamayan et al., 2007). Generally, an RTI model includes three levels of intervention (see Figure 7.1). The first two occur in the general classroom, and the third, the most intense, occurs when a student has been identified as having disabilities and special education services are provided. Li was provided with the first two tiers of interventions. These were part of the general classroom and included various specialists' responses to what was believed would be effective.

Figure 7.1 Three-Tiered Response to Intervention Model

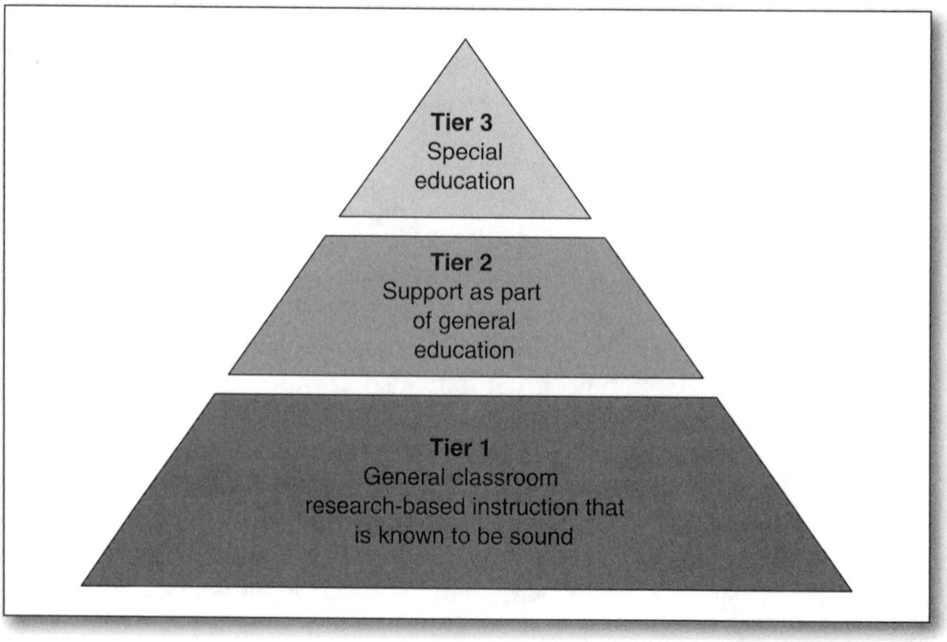

Tier 3
Special
education

Tier 2
Support as part
of general
education

Tier 1
General classroom
research-based instruction that
is known to be sound

According to the National Center on Response to Intervention (2010), there are four components to an RTI model:

- a school-wide, multi-level instructional and behavioral system for preventing school failure
- screening
- progress monitoring
- data-based decision making for instruction, movement within the multilevel system, and disability identification in accordance with state law (p. 1)

At the heart of an RTI model is making decisions that are based on actual data about individual student progress. The purpose of using actual data is to determine the students who may be at risk of doing poorly and, more important, providing them with interventions that are known to be effective. In this sense, an RTI model is intended to be a quick, deliberate, and proactive means for addressing potential failures *before they occur* by using interventions early on. It is also a means for better identifying students with disabilities so that appropriate interventions are applied to the students who need them. An RTI model also uses increasing levels of supports whereby students who indeed have disabilities receive the most support.

Many RTI models provide two levels of screenings at the beginning of the school year, or in the case of kindergarten, a prescreening, to identify the students who may be at risk of doing poorly (National Center on Response to Intervention, 2010). When the first level of screening is completed, a second screening occurs for those who have been identified in order to gather more information about students and to determine which ones are the most likely to struggle. In addition, some schools conduct this type of screening at different intervals during the same school year to best ensure that students at risk of failing will be identified before failure occurs and that appropriate interventions may be applied as needed. Student progress, in this sense, is monitored throughout the school year, and interventions are provided when needed. A true RTI model must ensure that its tests and measures of student progress and behavior are reliable and valid.

An RTI model must also utilize interventions that have been scientifically proven to be sound. They must be research based and known to be effective for the students for whom they are being used (National Center on Response to Intervention, 2010). When a student does not appear to respond, additional interventions must be applied. Generally, RTI models use increasing levels of intensity of support, from Tiers 1 to 3, as they are needed. Tier 3 support is used for students with identified learning disabilities (National Center on Response to Intervention, 2010).

As seen in Li's case example, her teacher and others provided interventions without referring Li for a special education evaluation. In addition, her programming for learning English was evaluated and strengthened. The following interventions or rapid responses were provided in Li's general education classes:

1. A bilingual translator was employed to help Li communicate with her peers and teacher.

2. Li had been receiving 20 minutes of ESL per week. Recognizing this as inadequate, the school increased the amount to an hour per day.

3. The school counselor worked with Li's parents.

4. The school counselor and psychologist provided support within Li's classroom to help her interact more appropriately with others.

Each of these responses supported Li in learning English and content and matriculating successfully to the first grade.

Factors to consider when using an RTI model with ELs

On the face of it, RTI may seem like an ideal model for providing the kind of individualized help that is needed when it is needed. It allows schools to provide interventions to students without the obstacle of having to wait for a special education evaluation to occur and be completed. This alone should make schools relieved, especially those that find waiting to refer an EL to be detrimental to the overall success of students. With all of these good reasons, why should schools be concerned about applying an RTI model with ELs? The viability of applying an RTI model with ELs demands our attention for many reasons:

- Some schools and states don't offer instruction or support in a student's primary language, have eliminated bilingual education programming, or have even abolished any programming in students' primary languages, making English the only language of instruction that is available for its ELs.
- Many schools have limited programming and resources for ELs. Rather than providing the most basic of programming for English language and content development, schools with limited services and staff provide much less than what is needed. As a result, ELs are not getting the type of programming that they should and do poorly because they are not provided with the type of basic educational programming to which they are entitled.
- Many of the actual interventions that are applied are not enough and/or do not address the specific needs of students from diverse linguistic and cultural experiences.
- Many ELs have had limited or interrupted prior schooling and are not afforded the time or specific instruction that is needed to learn literacy and grade-level content skills.

Thus, there are four primary reasons why English learners might not be any better off with an RTI model than without one. This is not to say that RTI is an ineffective model, rather, that it must be applied appropriately for ELs. Moreover, teaching ELs should mean that schools have a solid grounding in second language development and differences, the needed resources for teaching culturally and linguistically diverse students, and a depth of understanding about the specific cultures and cultural ways of being of students (Hoover et al., 2007). Fundamentally, schools' general education programming must be responsive to the varied linguistic and cultural representatives found among their ELs so that the students who struggle are not struggling due to inadequate programming.

A Tier 1 response is high-quality, scientifically proven general education programming

One of the core elements of Tier 1 of an RTI model is that the general educational programming for all learners is effective. An RTI model is heavily dependent on high-quality services being provided in the general education classroom and schools taking time to ensure that this is occurring. English language education (ELE) programming is not considered special education; it is part of the general education model. Creating effective programming for individual students means providing ELE programming that is scientifically known to be sound and effective with the supports that are needed for the ELs who are struggling. Most teachers have not been trained to teach ELs, and therefore, the decision to refer an EL for a special education evaluation is most likely being made by a teacher who has had little training to work with ELs. In addition, as seen earlier in this book, programming is often dictated by the availability of limited resources and not necessarily the needs of ELs. Indeed, programming for learning English and content may be inadequate.

A quick response sequence that is effective for the ELs who are struggling should be a top priority. As stated earlier, an RTI model must include a systematic gathering of data to determine the reasons why a student is experiencing challenges and identifying a set of individualized responses for addressing the challenges effectively. More important, rather than provide one type of intervention, multiple intervening steps, such as the ones employed with Li in the second example, can and should occur using an RTI model. However, how is a school to know what is best for ELs?

Gathering data to understand the effectiveness of ELE programming for the general population of ELs

Determining whether a student's difficulties are due to second language learning, a disability, or both is challenging for many districts. An important step is for a school to examine the effectiveness of its ELE programming.

Leaders must implement ELE programming models that are scientifically based and known to yield the best results. Chapters 2 and 3 provide school leaders with a synopsis of the related federal laws, regulations, and legal decisions (including the seminal *Castañeda v. Pickard*); programming models that have been found to be the most effective; and a means for selecting and applying the model that is the most appropriate for individual school circumstances. Leaders must also gather data about ELs who are struggling to learn in order to determine whether the difficulties that students are experiencing are due to the typical developmental process involved in learning English while also learning academic content or an underlying learning disability that occurs in both the home language and English. When difficulties are only seen in an English-only instructional context and not in the student's primary or home language, it is less likely that there is an underlying disability. When difficulties occur across all settings and in both languages, it is more likely that a referral for a special education evaluation may be an appropriate course of action (Hamayan et al., 2007).

Schools must examine the likelihood of ELs being referred as a result of inadequate programming or lack of understanding about the process of second language acquisition. That is, when students are placed in programs without, or with less than, the proper resources, it is far more likely that they will be referred for a special education evaluation and diagnosed with a special education disability. In Li's case, she had been provided with 30 minutes of weekly instruction in ESL—many times less than what was needed. Inadequate ELE programming is commonplace and must be remedied, if for nothing else, to relieve the disproportionate number of ELs who are misdiagnosed as having disabilities.

Examining the effectiveness of ELE programming and RTI with ELs

Careful examination of the frequency and reasons that ELs are and are not being referred can be very helpful. Such an evaluation greatly aids in understanding whether ELs are being referred due to external causes, such as ineffective programming or individual disabilities. Resource 7.1 provides school leaders with a format for this process.

School leaders should not wait for ELs to fail to launch into a tiered RTI model. There are many initial steps that leaders should routinely use to ensure that ELs are receiving effective programming.

Creating a data analysis team of ELE and special education staff

Implementing programming models that are scientifically proven to be sound is no guarantee that all students will do well or that a school will appropriately refer and evaluate students for potential disabilities. A systemic team approach is needed. School leaders should gather a team of specialists, special educators, ESL teachers, bilingual teachers, and parents for the purpose of analyzing the school's prereferral, referral, and disability services (see Resource 7.1). Using the results gathered from this evaluation, the team may discover that over- or underidentification is occurring because the ELE programming is underresourced (Hamayan et al., 2007). Remedies for this may involve doing the following:

- increasing professional development so that more teachers and specialists are trained and have a better understanding of the school's EL population from a cultural and linguistic perspective
- implementing daily ESL instruction so that students receive a greater continuum of English language development
- offering instruction or support in the student's home language so that students have increased access to the curriculum
- hiring more specialists who are bilingual and bicultural in students' home languages and cultures
- creating a districtwide approach to curriculum planning and delivery that includes an understanding of English language development and the importance of ELs' culture, language, and world experiences
- using a systemic team approach for evaluating the learning environment for ELs

Conducting an ongoing evaluation of the school's special education referral, identification, and services process for ELs and making modifications to ELE programming is an important means for strengthening the effectiveness of any ELE program. The purpose of the evaluation is to better ensure that students receive appropriate and effective programming for learning English and content, address the problem of a disproportionate number of ELs in special education, and ensure that ELs are more properly referred for special education evaluation and diagnosed with a special education disability. Once this is done, the immediate application of the following kinds of interventions, if warranted, is critical:

- providing help to individual students when they first appear to struggle to learn
- identifying the students who have disabilities
- supporting individual students with interventions that are proven to work
- evaluating the success of the supports and interventions so that additional or more intensive interventions may be applied if needed
- providing special education referral and service delivery

Ensuring equality for all students

When students are receiving quality core instruction and interventions as needed, they are more likely to be successful. The application of effective programming improves the outcomes for ELs. When these students are seen to be making progress, they are much less likely to be referred. Key to any quality program is collaboration. The rate of referral for ELs should be the same as it is for the general population of students. When students require a much higher level of intervention or modification, a special education referral may be needed. This should occur as a Tier 3 response.

The American Speech-Language-Hearing Association (ASHA; 1985) recognizes that not all speech and language therapists have the training and skills needed to serve ELs. It suggests that districts use a variety of strategies for evaluating and working with ELs. ASHA's suggestions are helpful for any specialist who is charged with evaluating and working with ELs.

First, reach out to schools, associations, and institutions to secure specialists that can be employed to evaluate and work with ELs. Colleges and universities are fine sources and resources for this work, as are professional associations, such as ASHA and the American Association for School Psychologists, as well as their state affiliates. Schools may find that recent graduates who are bilingual and bicultural can help with this important work. They may also find bilingual bicultural graduate students who need practicum experiences. This can be an ideal pairing for schools in need of this type of support. Reaching out to others is especially helpful for schools that need bilingual bicultural specialists who represent the same home languages as the schools' ELs.

Second, develop a collaborative or cooperative of districts. Collaboratives can be a fine means for finding specialists who can identify and work with ELs with disabilities. Educational service agencies can be particularly helpful in establishing collaboratives.[1]

Third, it may be helpful to secure a bilingual bicultural professional who is knowledgeable about the process of identifying and working with ELs with disabilities and can work closely with specialists. It is important for the specialist to review the testing that will take place and to receive input about its appropriateness for students from the particular language group for which it will be administered.

Finally, remediation or providing special education services should be considered an extension of the spectrum of interventions that have been provided to the student. It is important that the interventions provided be research based and known to be reliable for the ELs in question. The models that have been found to be the most successful, as stated in Chapters 2 and 3, are those that include the use of students' native language and respect for cultural differences and students' backgrounds.

Key to identifying and working with ELs with learning differences and learning disabilities is the quality of the programming and the means by which districts evaluate the effectiveness of that programming. In the next chapter, we will discuss making data-driven decisions based on effective measures of student performance.

---

[1]For information on educational service agencies in your area, visit the Association of Educational Service Agencies website at www.aesa.us.

RESOURCE 7.1
[School District] Evaluation of English Learners Referred for Special Education Evaluation and Diagnosed With a Disability

A team of English language and special education teachers and specialists should convene periodically to review and analyze data about the students who have been referred and evaluated for special education services.

Analysis of the EL Population

1. The total number of identified ELs in the school is _____.
   The total number of ELs who were referred during this school year for a special education evaluation in the school is _____. The total percentage of ELs referred for a special education evaluation during this school year is _____.

2. Is the proportion of ELs who have been *referred* the same as the proportion of the general population of students who have been referred? Yes ☐ No ☐ If no, what is the difference noted?

3. Is the proportion of ELs who have been *identified* as having disabilities the same as the proportion of the general population of students who have been identified? Yes ☐ No ☐ If no, describe the differences.

4. The languages spoken by the ELs in the school are:

5. The languages spoken by the ELs who were referred for a special education evaluation are:

6. Are there commonalities among the languages spoken by ELs and the reasons for referral or diagnosis of disability? Yes ☐ No ☐ If yes, what is the commonality?

Reasons That ELs Have Been Referred

7. The reasons, by total number of occurrence, that ELs were referred for a special education evaluation this year are:

_____ autism	_____ multiple disabilities	_____ speech/language impairment
_____ deaf-blindness		
_____ deafness	_____ orthopedic impairment	_____ traumatic brain injury
_____ emotional disturbance	_____ other health impairment	_____ visual impairment, including blindness
_____ hearing impairment		
_____ mental retardation	_____ specific learning disability	

8. The most common reason that ELs were referred for a special education evaluation this year is:

9. Anecdotally, describe any additional commonalities among the ELs who were referred (e.g., interrupted formal education).

Teachers and Specialists

10. Have the assessors been trained in second language acquisition and linguistic and cultural diversity? Yes ☐ No ☐ If no, what steps is the school taking to ensure that its evaluators, including school psychologists, speech and language therapists, and special education staff, are being trained?

Assessments

11. Do the assessments used to identify ELs with disabilities make use of relevant and actual behaviors in classroom contexts? Yes ☐ No ☐

12. Are assessments being provided in the students' home language by staff who have trained in second language acquisition and practices for teaching ELs? Yes ☐ No ☐ If no, what steps has the school taken to ensure that actual data are used?

ELE Programming Services

13. Do the ELs who have been referred receive effective programming for learning English, including:

   a. An English language development program from a licensed ESL teacher? Yes ☐ No ☐

   b. An appropriate amount of daily instruction of English language development for ELs? Yes ☐ No ☐

   c. Content instruction from a teacher who is trained to teach ELs? Yes ☐ No ☐

   d. Curriculum that is specifically connected to ELs' personal, cultural, linguistic, and world experiences and knowledge so that it is meaningful, relevant, and comprehensible? Yes ☐ No ☐

   e. An education program for students with interrupted formal education? Yes ☐ No ☐.

14. If any of the responses to Question 13 are "no," what steps is the school taking to ensure that its programming for ELs is properly resourced?

REFERENCES

American Speech-Language-Hearing Association. (1985). *Clinical management of communicatively handicapped minority language populations* [Position Statement]. Retrieved December 23, 2010, from http://www.asha.org/docs/html/PS1985-00219.html

Artiles, A., & Ortiz. A. (Eds.). (2002). *English language learners with special education needs: Assessment, identification, and instruction.* Washington, DC: Center for Applied Linguistics.

Artiles, A. J., Trent, S. C., & Palmer, J. (2004). Culturally diverse students in special education: Legacies and prospects. In J. A. Banks & C. M. Banks (Eds.), *Handbook of research on multicultural education* (2nd ed., pp. 716–735). San Francisco: Jossey-Bass.

Baca, L. (1990) Theory and practice in bilingual/cross cultural special education: Major issues and implications for research, practice, and policy. In *Proceedings of the First Research Symposium on Limited English Proficient Student Issues* (pp. 247–280). Washington, DC: U.S. Department of Education, Office of Bilingual Education and Minority Language Affairs. Retrieved May 17, 2010: http://www.ncela.gwu.edu/files/rcd/BE018297/1st_Symposium_Theory.pdf

Donovan, S., & Cross, C. (2002). *Minority students in special and gifted education.* Washington, DC: National Academy Press.

Esparza Brown, J., & Doolittle, J. (2008). *A cultural, linguistic, and ecological framework for response to intervention with English language learners.* Tempe, AZ: National Center for Culturally Responsive Educational Systems.

Fuchs, D., Mock, D., Morgan, P. L., & Young, C. L. (2003). Responsiveness-to-intervention: Definitions, evidence, and implications for the learning disabilities construct. *Learning Disabilities Research & Practice, 18*(3), 157–171.

Haager, D., Klingner, J. K., & Vaughn, S. (Eds.). (2007). *Validated reading practices for three tiers of intervention.* Baltimore: Brookes.

Hamayan, E., Marler, B., Sanchez Lopez, C., & Damico, J. (2007). *Special education considerations for English language learners: Delivering a continuum of services.* Philadelphia: Caslon.

Haynes, J., & Zacarian, D. (2010). *Teaching English language learners across the content areas.* Alexandria, VA: Association for Supervision and Curriculum Development.

Hoover, J., Klingner, J., Baca, L., & Patton, J. (2007). *Methods for teaching culturally and linguistically diverse exceptional learners.* New York: Merrill/Prentice Hall.

Klingner, J. K., & Edwards, P. A. (2006). Cultural considerations with response to intervention models. *Reading Research Quarterly, 41*(1), 108–117.

National Center on Response to Intervention. (2010). *Essential components of RTI: A closer look at response to intervention.* Washington, DC: U.S. Department of Education, Office of Special Education Programs, National Center on Response to Intervention. Retrieved December 23, 2010, from http://www.rti4success.org/images/stories/pdfs/rtiessentialcomponents_042710.pdf

National Dissemination Center for Children with Disabilities. (2009). *Categories of disabilities under IDEA.* Washington, DC: Author. Retrieved December 23, 2010, from http://www.nichcy.org/disabilities/categories/pages

8

Making Data-Driven Decisions Based on Effective Measures of Student Performance

When secondary school principal Mr. Ross analyzed the performance of his ninth-grade students on the state's annual assessment of English, he noted that the English learners (ELs) had not made annual yearly progress—again. As a subgroup, many had scored well below the school's average. As he began to analyze the data, he found that the ELs had done poorly on each of the subtests, and he could not find anything specific enough to determine a strategy for improving their progress. At the end of a half hour (the only time that he had during what promised to be a busy day), Mr. Ross surmised that the primary reason for the ELs' poor performance was the type of teaching that had occurred. He decided to meet with their ESL teacher, Mrs. Fernandez, to determine what might be going awry in her classes.

First, Mr. Ross decided to observe her teaching. He noted that her students seemed engaged in the poem that they were analyzing and that she used information from each student's personal life to help him or her make a connection to the poem's meaning. After the class bell rang and the students had left, he told Mrs. Fernandez about her students' performance on the English language arts section of the state assessment.

"You can't really expect them to score well," she responded. "After all, they are not fluent enough in English to take the test and do well on it."

Thinking that this was a logical answer, Mr. Ross decided it wasn't worth looking closely at the state assessment as the data were likely incomplete and irrelevant. He wasn't quite sure if this was a good or bad approach, however, and began considering the ways he might learn more about the ELs and their performance in his school.

Improving student outcomes is an important goal for all school leaders and is particularly important regarding ELs because the nation's schools, as a whole, have not been very successful in educating these students. Indeed, as discussed in Chapter 1, the achievement gap between ELs and the general population of students continues to be significant and continues to grow (Zehr, 2009). For example, according to the U.S. Department of Education (2007), ELs scored half as well as the general population in reading and math. Outcomes such as this speak to the need to make data-driven decisions that are based on ways in which student performance will improve. In other words, making informed decisions about instructional programming for ELs must be intentionally focused on improving their outcome.

Federal and some state laws and regulations require schools to set improvement standards and determine what needs to be done to achieve them. Under the No Child Left Behind Act (NCLB), school improvement plans are often based on the results of state and local assessments. School leaders typically analyze testing results with the goal of finding the areas in which students performed poorly and identifying the students who did so. State reporting systems look at how a whole group does (by state, district, and school) and, under NCLB, are required to disaggregate assessment data to provide information about specific subgroups of students (U.S. Department of Education, 2007). Some school leaders disaggregate the data further to learn more about student responses to specific questions and groups within subgroups (e.g., Cambodian and Chinese students within an Asian subgroup). Using this information, leaders typically create a plan for improving their testing outcomes. For example, it is not uncommon for schools to create state assessment preparation classes in their efforts to help certain student groups to perform better.

Analysis of subgroup performance is intended to help school leaders, teachers, and others better understand ways for improving the conditions by which specific groups of students, such as ELs, can learn best. Armed with this information, it is expected that administrators and other stakeholders will successfully determine *who* needs to improve, *what* needs to be improved, and *how* improvement might be accomplished. On the face of it, this sounds like a fairly straightforward task. That is, interpreting assessment data will result in securing the "right" steps that are needed for making improvements. Unfortunately, the cycle of poring over state data continues and has not yielded much in the way of positive results. Why is this?

First, few school leaders have been trained to analyze data and make data-driven decisions (Elmore, 2002; Wayman, Midgley, & Stringfield, 2006). Against much evidence to the contrary, it is expected that they have the capacity (including the preparation and time) to take student assessment data and magically turn it into understandable and usable information for improving the planning and delivery of lessons and the performance outcomes of students (Wayman et al., 2006). Second, as we learned in Chapter 1, few leaders have been trained to work with linguistically and culturally diverse learners, nor do they have direct experience teaching them. As a result, they are charged with studying and addressing the outcomes of a group on which they have little educational background and a limited experiential frame from which to draw. Third, ELs, as we also learned in Chapter 1, are not a monolithic subgroup. Some have had prior schooling experiences that are similar to their experiences in their current school, while others have not. Some are literate in their home language; others are not. Many live in poverty. The list of differences among ELs goes on and on, making it difficult for an accurate analysis of state measures to be possible, even by the most seasoned of administrators. Thus, for many reasons, making decisions based on state assessment outcomes is not an easily accomplished task.

In this chapter, we will explore a variety of means for understanding student performance as it relates to ELs. We will explore the following question: What are fair and equitable assessment evaluation practices of ELs and their programming? We will also identify better ways for using state measures to understand their strengths and weaknesses and, using an asset-based instructional model, developing strategies to better address student outcomes. In addition, we will explore using local formative and summative assessments to measure EL achievement and English language education (ELE) program effectiveness. Finally, we will learn about designing rubrics and monitoring charts to effectively measure student performance, parent involvement, and community-building efforts.

WHAT ARE FAIR AND EQUITABLE ASSESSMENT EVALUATION PRACTICES OF ELS AND THEIR PROGRAMMING?

High-stakes tests are those by which teachers and administrators are held accountable for students' performance. They are referred to as *high-stakes tests* because so much depends on their outcome. For example, students have the right to attend an alternative school when their school does not make Adequate Yearly Progress (AYP) for two consecutive years

(U.S. Department of Education, 2009). There are additional measures that can be taken when schools do not make AYP on state assessments, some of which are much more extreme than students attending an alternative school. Indeed, everyone can be hurt when a school's overall performance on statewide tests is poor. Schools can suffer the loss of funding, and school leaders and teachers can lose their jobs (Coltrane, 2002). Students can also suffer greatly at the cost of being denied a high school diploma, grade promotion, and other highly important expectations and milestones. With all of this at stake, are high-stakes tests fair and reasonable—particularly for ELs? While the initial intent of NCLB was to raise the quality of learning environments so that everyone would succeed and no one would be left behind, the nation's EL achievement gap speaks to the need to look more closely at the positive and negative implications of high-stakes testing.

Prior to the passage of NCLB in 2001, ELs were not required to take state exams during their first three years of learning English. As a result, few were administered high-stakes tests (Abeldi & Dietel, 2004; Coltrane, 2002). There were positive and negative implications associated with this flexibility. One positive implication was that ELs were not penalized for their lack of English. Important milestones such as grade-to-grade promotions and graduation were not affected. Students could continue to move from one grade to the next without needing to worry whether their ability to complete school and/or a grade hinged on their performance on a high-stakes test. Some negative implications stemming from the lack of accountability were that many ELs (1) were left to languish without much needed support, (2) were not considered in the overall planning and delivery of instruction and programming, (3) were promoted from one grade to the next or given a high school diploma without providing them with the academic and language development to which they were entitled, and (4) dropped out of school (Abeldi & Dietel, 2004; Coltrane, 2002).

The advent of NCLB meant that all students, including ELs, were to be held to the same standard. There are positives about this law. It has made some schools that had not been accountable for its ELs accountable for them. It also provides schools with information about the progress of their ELs and requires schools to pay attention to this population.

On the negative side, and there are many negatives, ELs are taking tests that are designed, normed, validated, and administered for the general population, that is, monolingual speakers of American English. The tests are not targeted to the complex needs of a culturally and linguistically diverse population (Abeldi & Dietel, 2004; Coltrane, 2002). And test questions can be culturally biased. For example, many ELs come from countries that use the metric system and are not familiar with U.S. customary units of measurement. A math question that requires these ELs to express a solution in feet and inches is problematic because they have not been reared using this system. Their failure to respond correctly to such a question is more likely to be because of cultural bias or barrier as opposed to lack of mathematical knowledge. In addition, many ELs may not be familiar with the context of the questions. Let's look at another math example involving expansion and extension. In this one, students are provided with an example using orange juice concentrate and are asked how many cans it will take to make a quart of juice. Unless students know what *concentrate* means in this specific question, they may be totally stumped. And there are countless other such examples.

Being required to take these high-stakes tests in English puts ELs at a distinct disadvantage in measuring their capacity to demonstrate and express an understanding of academic content. An all-too-common outcome is that the test results are too challenging for them, their parents, educators, and other stakeholders to understand and interpret well (Coltrane, 2002). Further, high-stakes tests can and do prevent some students from being promoted and graduating high school because they cannot perform on a test that is entirely administered in English. Poor testing results can also lead to placing students in classes that are far below their academic abilities. This includes remedial classes and, for some students, being referred for a special education evaluation, which can lead to being inappropriately identified as having a disability. In response, some states offer Spanish versions of portions of their state exams. While this sounds like an important remedy, it has many flaws. For instance, Massachusetts passed a law in 2002 that required most of the state's schools to use an English-only model of instruction, which means that the students who take portions of the state assessment in Spanish are not likely to be in classrooms where the language of instruction is in Spanish. As such, they are not as well prepared to take the test as are their English-fluent peers.

Fair and equitable testing for ELs involves allowing students to demonstrate their knowledge of English *and* content. Test developers must acknowledge, and have depth of understanding, that ELs are learning a second language simultaneously while learning content. Second language and academic learning are not mutually exclusive. When American English–fluent students are tested, the demands on them are less challenging than they are for ELs because they know the language, context, and culture. Equity can only occur when careful accommodations are made for ELs. Typically, ELs may be given more time to take a test or be tested in a setting in which they are more comfortable (Coltrane, 2002). These supports alone will not ensure that the tests can actually measure ELs' performance accurately. Their lack of English can diminish their ability to demonstrate what they know. Their lack of contextual and cultural knowledge can also significantly impact their performance. While it can be helpful to test students in their native language, this prospect presupposes that students are also learning in their native language, that they are being instructed about the culture and context in which the test question is targeted, and that the test reflects what has been taught and learned. Thus, fair and equitable testing of ELs is complex and not easily realized.

USING A FOUR-PRONGED APPROACH

One approach for improving student performance is to look at the types of learning environments that are likely to yield the best results and testing that can capture ELs' language and academic development. Language learning is not purely learning language, and content learning is not merely learning content. A helpful means for understanding the process of language and content learning is to look closely at the four interdependent components that were presented in Chapters 4 and 5:

1. Learning is a sociocultural process.
2. Learning is a developmental process.
3. Learning is an academic process.
4. Learning is a cognitive process.

Data-based decisions regarding the curriculum and lesson planning and delivery should take into account these components. When this is done, school leaders have a much better awareness of what is important to consider and include.

Learning is a sociocultural process

Learning is personal. It is dependent on our ability to connect what is to be learned with our personal, social, cultural, and world knowledge. Our capacity to learn is directly related to our ability to connect what is to be learned with our familiarity to the context in which it is situated. For example, the concept of war has powerful personal meanings for some individuals. People who have personally experienced living in a war-torn country have a much different perspective than those that have not. The former are able to connect their personal, cultural, and world knowledge to the concepts being taught about war. The latter are dependent on their teacher, peers, and others to make learning meaningful.

Let's look at a second example. In a school play, the declaration "I now pronounce you husband and wife" is stated. Because it is a familiar social event and context, indeed a sociocultural event, we can surmise a good deal. First, the person who is stating this declaration likely has the power to engage two parties in a marital contract, such as a minister. The statement is likely occurring in a particular location such as a church, city hall, or other place at which weddings occur. The declaration is also being stated in front of at least two people, and maybe more. Thus, the short sentence is packed with social and cultural meaning. However, it is only comprehensible if the listener is familiar with the social context of a wedding ceremony.

In a great sense, ELs are dependent on their teachers to make the context relevant and meaningful. In addition, learning is a social process that involves a high level of interaction. Pair and group work are important methods to use and are only successful when explicit instruction is given for engaging in this type of work. The absence of these connection-making activities can be a significant reason why some students are disconnected from the learning process and parents are disconnected from their child's school. Social and cultural contexts are highly relevant for making decisions about the curriculum, lesson planning and delivery, the school environment, and the community as a whole. Quality learning and school community environments and experiences must take into account the sociocultural process.

Learning is a developmental process

Language learning is a developmental process, and it consists of four domains: listening, speaking, reading, and writing. It involves being able to comprehend and produce language fluently, use a wide range of vocabulary, pronounce words so that they are easily understood, and use grammar appropriately for the situation. The process of learning a second language does not occur overnight. Rather, it is a developmental process that involves a high level of mastery of these comprehension and production elements. It is typical for beginning language learners, for example, to utter one to two words to signal meaning and more advanced learners to use complete sentences with perhaps a few grammatical errors that do not interfere with meaning. Making data-driven decisions about ELs must take into account that language learning is a developmental process, and tests, whether high stakes or otherwise, must reflect this process. In practice, it means that educators and administrators must understand the English proficiency levels of their students and match the instructional program and assessments with these levels.

Learning is an academic process

Academic learning spans all of the content areas. Language arts, math, science, technology, social studies, and all other subject matter are intended to be expanded and extended as students move from one grade to the next. As students move up the grades, their vocabulary grows, as do their sociolinguistic, sociocultural, and cognitive academic capacities (Collier, 1995). What is learned in one language can be transferred to a second language, and that is why, fundamentally, it is believed that the most efficient and effective means for learning a new language is to do so while continuing to develop academically (Collier, 1995; Goldenberg & Coleman, 2010; Francis, Lesaux, & August, 2006). While some might believe that it is better to delay the learning of content in favor of allocating time for learning English, the opposite is true. Students learn best when they can continue to develop socioculturally, linguistically, academically, and cognitively.

Learning is a cognitive process

Learning is more than mastering the curriculum. It involves the capacity to use a high level of thinking skills appropriately. For example, let's look at a third-grade classroom in which the teacher tells her students, "Get in your groups." She does this on a routine basis and punctuates the command by turning the lights on and off in her classroom. The prompt *get in your groups* is filled with meaning. On a simple level, students need to remember to stop doing what they are doing and listen to their teacher. However, the command actually requires students to do much more:

- Stop doing what they are doing.
- Listen carefully to what the teacher commands.
- Process this information.
- Transition from what they are doing to get into their groups.
- Engage in group work.

Thus, the command *get in your groups* requires students to remember, understand, and apply a specific type of information and use it when responding to this command. Some students seem to follow the remembering, understanding, and applying steps easily, whereas others do not. What is important is that these thinking skills must be taught explicitly so that *all* students have the capacity to engage in high-level thinking. Drawing from Bloom's taxonomy (Forehand, 2005; Bloom & Krathwohl, 1956), the type of thinking skills that are needed to be successful in school and elsewhere fall into six distinct categories of increasing levels of complexity (Anderson & Krathwohl, 2001):

1. Remembering

2. Understanding

3. Applying

4. Analyzing

5. Evaluating

6. Creating

Let's look at another classroom in which a teacher has required her students to create a graphic organizer to illustrate key ideas about the causes of the Civil War. To complete the task successfully, a student must have knowledge about the following:

- the key causes of the Civil War
- cause-effect relationships

- the types of organizers that might be used to describe a cause-effect relationship
- how to create a graphic organizer that illustrates key causes of the Civil War

In the range of complexity, this is a fairly complex task that requires much more than remembering, understanding, and applying. Students must also engage in the cognitive tasks of analyzing, evaluating, and creating. Each task and assignment requires a different level of complexity or thinking skill. These are not learned in a vacuum. High-quality learning environments are those in which educators explicitly teach cognitive processing skills so that learning can occur for everyone.

Thus, language learning involves the presence of four interdependent components: sociocultural, language, academic, and cognitive. Each supports the learning process. School leaders must ensure that each of these four components is implemented routinely and consistently. The absence of any one can be detrimental to the overall development and success of ELs.

USING LOCAL FORMATIVE AND SUMMATIVE ASSESSMENTS TO MEASURE EL ACHIEVEMENT AND ELE PROGRAM EFFECTIVENESS

Evaluating the success of any program has to be a multidimensional process to comprehensively take into account the whole student and the diversity found among students. Using the four-pronged sociocultural, language, academic, and cognitive approach is a helpful means for securing the type of information that is needed for making decisions about programming as well as student achievement.

Whether it is to determine the successful delivery of a lesson as it is occurring, a unit of study after it has occurred, or even a parent conference, a good approach is to ensure that ELs' sociocultural, language, academic, and cognitive needs are being met. There are two means for engaging in this type of assessment: formative and summative.

It is commonplace for school leaders, teachers, and other educators to continuously assess the effectiveness of an event, such as a lesson, as it is occurring. This on-the-spot type of formative assessment allows educators to make immediate shifts and changes as they are needed. Let's look at Mr. Stebbins's social studies class as it is unfolding. He begins the day's lesson by asking, "Does anyone know the causes of the Civil War?" In response, there is silence. Quickly realizing that his students are not going to respond, he immediately alters his plan. He tells a short story about his family's background. He tells the class that his family had once been slaves in Louisiana, where they were forced to work from sunrise to sunset six days a week. He says that his grandfather used to tell him stories about what it was like for his family to live as slaves. He then poses the question, "Have you or anyone you have known lived in slavery?" He then asks his students to talk with a partner about the question. Afterward, he walks around the classroom and carefully listens to his students' responses. When he hears some fall off task, he quietly walks over and helps them return to the assignment. Using this type of formative assessment provides Mr. Stebbins with a safety net to check for understanding and to make the changes that are needed to ensure that his students are engaged in learning.

Formative assessment provides opportunities to individualize instruction and support the comprehension and application of content. Think of the example used earlier, in which a teacher required her students to use a graphic organizer to describe the key causes of the Civil War. Aside from the obvious task that has been assigned, high-quality plans and instruction build students' capacity to learn meaningfully by connecting content and lesson delivery with students' personal, social, cultural, and world knowledge. High-quality lesson plans and instruction also require that the task match the current English proficiency level of students, that it be academic, and that the cognitive skills that are needed be explicitly instructed. Thus, by launching a four-pronged approach, educators have a much better means for delivering lessons that meet the needs of their ELs and making changes as they are needed.

The same is true for summative assessments. These are used after a unit of study is completed or a certain time period has passed (e.g., the end of term) to determine how much learning has taken place. They can also occur in the form of a state assessment to ensure that certain standards have been met. What is critical is that students receive an explicit instructional program that is connected to their personal lives (the sociocultural prong), their level of English proficiency (the language prong), their content learning needs (the academic prong), and, finally, the thinking skills that are needed in order to take summative assessments (the cognitive prong). Thus the data that guide decisions must be focused on these four interdependent lenses.

SELECTING A COLLABORATIVE GROUP TO UNDERSTAND ELs' ACADEMIC PERFORMANCE AND NEEDS

Unfortunately, educators can make significant errors in determining the needs of their students and the curriculum (Love, Stiles, Mundry, & DiRanna, 2008; Wayman et al., 2006). This is particularly true in relation to ELs since most school leaders and teachers have had no training in working with this growing population. While this is a problem, it is not without solutions. An important first step is for school leaders to consider the possibility of involving a team in the analysis process as opposed to making it a solo proposition. Knowing that school leaders have not been trained to analyze data and work with culturally and linguistically diverse students, gathering a team to engage in this work may help transform this into a collaborative instead of solo process. It speaks to the heart of a school or district's responsibility. ELs need to be considered everyone's students and a shared responsibility. To do this requires a collaborative look at how

- the curriculum and materials used to teach students connect with their personal, cultural, world, and academic experiences;
- the materials and delivery of lessons connect with ELs' language learning needs;
- the method used will achieve the academic goals;
- cognitive skills are taught; and, most important,
- effective the curriculum and delivery of lessons are with ELs.

Love et al. (2008) describe the importance of this being a collaborative process. Thought must be given to how many and who should be engaged in this collaboration to ensure that appropriate analysis and plans are made for a school or district's ELs. Ideally, collaborative groups should consist of six to eight people. This allows for a wide range of participants and at the same time is a small-enough group to ensure that everyone is an active member and has an important role to play.

The ideal behind a collaborative group is to better ensure a deeper understanding about a school's EL population and their learning needs. It is critical that the group's members represent the diversity found among the EL population. For example, a school may select a Spanish-speaking world language teacher, figuring that the teacher speaks the language of its ELs. Yet speaking the language is not enough. Selecting a bilingual bicultural representative of the EL population is highly important. The more "insider" information is collected, the more likely it is that appropriate and effective educational plans and delivery will occur. Thus, in this important process, school leaders must include staff and community members who are familiar with their EL population. That is, they must include ESL, bilingual, and classroom teachers who work with ELs and, most important, key informants who are members of or familiar with ELs' personal, cultural, language, and prior schooling experiences.

The absence of this key insider/informant role may lead groups astray. For example, let's say that a subgroup of ELs is underperforming in math. A bilingual bicultural faculty member may know that the tasks and assignments that are given to students do not reflect the background experiences of ELs and that the cultural mismatch is what is causing poor performance. This insider knowledge greatly helps in securing a more culturally neutral and appropriate instructional approach. Similarly, a key member of a language and cultural group can help the collaborative team identify the cognitive skills that may be needed.

For example, let's look at Alberto, who failed the state assessment in math. When a collaborative team analyzed his performance, they found that he had skipped several questions. Without the participation of a bilingual bicultural member, the team may assume that Alberto did not possess the mathematical knowledge that he needed to be successful and may recommend that he repeat the math course. However, a member of the same language and cultural group as Alberto knew that he came from a culture in which making an educated guess was not a norm. He knew that when Alberto was not absolutely sure of the answer, it was a norm that he should not respond to the question. Armed with this cultural information, Alberto's math teacher helped him learn the process and rationale for making an educated guess, and Alberto passed the subsequent state math assessment with ease.

COLLABORATIVELY EXAMINING THE NEEDS OF ELs BY FIRST LOOKING AT THE WHOLE STUDENT COMMUNITY

Choosing what should be examined is as important as deciding who should be involved in the team engaged in the examination process. It is important to know how a school, grade, or class performs as a whole to have a good idea about its strengths and potential productive challenges. It is equally important to avoid assumptions about a curriculum or the methodology used to deliver it. For example, a school may believe that the curriculum series it purchased is of high quality because it includes supplemental materials for an EL population. However, the supplement is no guarantee that it will be successful as it may not be targeted for the particular group of ELs at that school.

Assembling a description of current ELs

In Chapter 1, we learned that some ELs have prior literacy and schooling experiences that match those of their current school. We also learned that the majority of the nation's ELs come from non-literacy-oriented backgrounds, that many come from culturally disrupted backgrounds, and that the majority live in poverty. Ascertaining whether the ELs in a school or district are from literacy-oriented, non-literacy-oriented, or culturally disrupted backgrounds is critical.

An important first task for the collaborative group is to gather knowledge about the school's ELs so that the group has specific and relevant information. Chapter 3 includes a variety of documents intended for the chick will hatch. Each of these skills—observe, track, and predict—involves a variety of thinking skills that should be included in rubrics for measuring student performance. They should also be part of any observational or other supervisory rubric for measuring the effectiveness of the curriculum and teachers' use of explicit instruction of cognitive skills.

Let's visit Mrs. Park's kindergarten class to see how her school developed its rubric and monitoring charts for its science unit on animals that lay eggs. The content standard for the unit of study is that students will demonstrate an understanding of the concept of egg-laying animals. Mrs. Park has 18 students in her classroom. Twelve are native speakers of American English; four are Spanish-speaking ELs from Mexico, El Salvador, and Honduras; one is a Yoruba-speaking EL from Nigeria, and one is a Japanese-speaking EL. All of the ELs are at the Starting level of learning English; they are beginning to utter one or two words in English. At many schools, teachers such as Mrs. Park would find it challenging to create and deliver a unit of study for a heterogeneous group composed of American English–fluent students and ELs. However, Mrs. Park's school has taken into account its diverse population.

The curriculum unit was developed by a collaborative team of kindergarten, ESL, and bilingual teachers as well as community members, all under the leadership of the district's curriculum director. Their meetings included four foci to develop the unit. The first concentrated on the academic goals of the unit. The second concentrated on the ways in which students' prior personal, cultural, and world knowledge experiences would be used to build connections with the content. The third concentrated on the cognitive skills that students would learn while engaging in the unit. The fourth focused on the means by which students would communicate the language of the content, including how Starting, or preproduction, ELs would be expected to communicate.

When Mrs. Park consulted her district's science curriculum guide on this unit of study, she reviewed the various rubrics and monitor charts that had been created. The rubrics were separated into four foci to ensure that she would address the four interdependent elements and be inclusive of her ELs. The overarching goals of the curriculum guide stated that teachers must build lessons focused on the following:

1. Learning is a sociocultural process.
   a. Educators must build explicit connections to students' personal, cultural, and world experiences in the teaching of curriculum.
   b. Educators must support students in learning about the social and cultural expectations of our classrooms, schools, district, and community.
2. Learning is a developmental process.
   a. Learning to communicate effectively involves listening, speaking, reading, and writing.

b. Educators must target instruction and assessments to the developmental levels of each of their students, including ELs who are at various stages of English proficiency.

3. Learning is an academic process.
   a. Each unit of study must have clear curriculum goals and objectives.
   b. Educators must support students in learning the curriculum and demonstrating an understanding of it.

4. Learning is a cognitive process.
   a. Learning involves the development of thinking skills.
   b. The specific thinking skills that are to be used in a content area must be explicitly taught.

A rubric and monitoring chart can be a helpful means for measuring the effectiveness of learning environments as well as family-school engagement efforts. Resources 8.1 and 8.2 provide suggested monitoring charts for this purpose. Coupled with Resource 5.1 in Chapter 5, these are intended to identify what is going well and what is in need of improvement.

The charts can be used by collaborative teams, coaches, peers, and supervisors. Ideally, they should be used at least four times per year to ensure routine measures of what is actually occurring. However, four observations are no guarantee that practices leading to successful student outcomes and school-family engagement will occur. A more helpful means for this type of transformative work is a peer-coaching model. Peer coaching encourages the type of reflection that is needed for engaging in the observational activities outlined in Resources 8.1 and 8.2. This model can provide ideal opportunities for grade-alike and subject-alike peers to learn with and from each other. Ongoing communication among colleagues has the power to improve overall student outcomes because it allows educators to discuss, reflect, and refine their practice together (Boatright & Galluci, 2008). Resources 8.1 and 8.2 are also helpful supervisory tools. Additionally, continuous monitoring on a routine basis is essential for making data-driven decisions that are intentionally focused on successful student outcomes and a high level of family-school engagement.

Indeed, transforming schools for English learners requires that leaders understand the changing dynamics of this population, the regulations governing their education, staff preparedness to design and deliver high-quality English language instruction and content programming, importance of parent engagement, and the power of a collaborative process in examining and strengthening schools' efforts. When this occurs, rural, suburban, and urban school leaders with low and high incidences of culturally and linguistically diverse student populations can build a school environment in which English learners can flourish.

3. Routine social events are conducted throughout the year to explicitly support EL parent involvement by paying particular attention to ELs' and their families' personal, cultural, language, and world experiences. ☐ ☐ ☐ ☐

4. Routine events, including parent interviews, occur to support school understanding about ELs' and parents' prior schooling and school involvement experiences. ☐ ☐ ☐ ☐

5. School leaders and teachers work together to create and sustain a welcoming environment for ELs and their families. ☐ ☐ ☐ ☐

Comments:

School-community efforts reflect the English proficiency levels of the EL parent and family community.

6. The home language survey and other means are used to identify the parents who need oral and/or written translations. ☐ ☐ ☐ ☐

7. Bilingual bicultural outreach is provided as needed. ☐ ☐ ☐ ☐

Comments:

Parent involvement is connected to their child's learning.

8. Parent activities are connected with their child's learning. ☐ ☐ ☐ ☐

9. Learning is explicitly connected to ELs' family and community experiences. ☐ ☐ ☐ ☐

10. EL parents are furnished with information about their child's educational program and goals in meaningful and comprehensible ways. ☐ ☐ ☐ ☐

11. EL parents are intentionally supported to learn about their child's educational program in meaningful and comprehensible ways. ☐ ☐ ☐ ☐

Comments:

REFERENCES

Abeldi, J., & Dietel, R. (2004). *Challenges in the No Child Left Behind Act for English language learners.* Los Angeles: University of California, Los Angeles, National Center for Research on Evaluation, Standards, and Student Testing. Retrieved December 27, 2010, from http://www.cse.ucla.edu/products/policy/cresst_policy7.pdf

Anderson, L. W., & Krathwohl, D. R. (Eds.). (2001). *A taxonomy for learning, teaching and assessing: A revision of Bloom's taxonomy of educational objectives.* New York: Longman.

Bloom, B. S., & Krathwohl, D. R. (1956). *Taxonomy of educational objectives: The classification of educational goals, by a committee of college and university examiners. Handbook 1: Cognitive domain.* New York: Longman.

Boatright, B., & Galluci, C. (with Swanson, J., Van Lare, M., & Yoon, I.). (2008). Coaching for instructional improvement: Themes in research and practice. *Washington State Kappan, 2*(1), 3–5. Retrieved December 27, 2010, from http://depts.washington.edu/uwcel/resources/papers/kappan_article1.pdf

Chamot, A. U., & O'Malley, J. M. (2009). The CALLA handbook: Implementing the Cognitive Academic Language Learning Approach (2nd ed.). New York: Pearson.

Collier, V. (1995). Acquiring a second language for school. *Directions in Language & Education, 1*(4). Retrieved July 13, 2010, from http://qcpages.qc.cuny.edu/ECP/bilingualcenter/Newsletters/Acquiring2ndLangV3-1.pdf

Coltrane, B. (2002). English language learners and high-stakes tests: an overview of the issues. *ERIC Digest.* Retrieved December 27, 2010, from http://www.cal.org/resources/digest/0207coltrane.html

Elmore, R. F. (2002). *Bridging the achievement gap between standards and achievement: The imperative for professional development in education.* Washington, DC: Albert Shanker Institute.

Forehand, M. (2005). Bloom's taxonomy: Original and revised. In M. Orey (Ed.), *Emerging perspectives on learning, teaching, and technology.* Retrieved December 27, 2010, from http://projects.coe.uga.edu/epltt/index.php?title=Bloom%27s_Taxonomy

Francis, D. J., Lesauz, N. K., August, D. (2006). Language of instruction. In D. August & T. Shanahan (Eds.), *Developing literacy in second-language learners: Report of the National Literacy Panel of Language Minority Children and Youth* (pp. 365–413). Mahwah, NJ: Lawrence Erlbaum.

Goldenberg, C., & Coleman, R. (2010). *Promoting academic achievement among English learners: A guide to the research.* Thousand Oaks, CA: Corwin.

Love, N., Stiles, K. E., Mundry, S., & DiRanna, K. (2008). *The data coach's guide to improving learning for all students: Unleashing the power of collaborative inquiry.* Thousand Oaks, CA: Corwin.

U.S. Department of Education. (2004). Subpart 2: Accountability and administration. Retrieved January 16, 2011, from http://www2.ed.gov/policy/elsec/leg/esea02/pg42.html#sec3121

U.S. Department of Education. (2007). *State and local implementation of the No Child Left Behind Act: Volume III—Accountability under NCLB.* Retrieved December 27, 2010, from http://www2.ed.gov/rschstat/eval/disadv/nclb-accountability/nclb-accountability.pdf

U.S. Department of Education. (2009). *No Child Left Behind: A toolkit for teachers.* Retrieved December 27, 2010, from http://www2.ed.gov/teachers/nclbguide/nclb-teachers-toolkit.pdf

Wayman, J. C., Midgley, S., & Stringfield, S. (2006). *Leadership for data-based decision-making: Collaborative educator teams.* Paper presented at the Annual Meeting of the American Education Research Association, San Francisco. Retrieved December 27, 2010, from http://edadmin.edb.utexas.edu/datause/papers/Wayman-Midgley-Stringfield-AERA2006.pdf

Zehr, M. A. (2009). Adopted tongue: English language learners pose policy puzzle. *Quality Counts, 28*(17), 8–9.

Glossary

Additive Bilingual Education: A program model focused on developing and maintaining a student's native language and English. The primary goal is for students to achieve high levels of literacy in both languages. Additive types include *dual-language, bilingual maintenance, two-way,* and *heritage language* programs.

Adequate Yearly Progress (AYP): Per the federal No Child Left Behind Act, a minimum level of performance that students in each school and school district must achieve on an annual basis. English learners are included in this requirement.

Aggregate Data: Generally, the population as a whole in reference to a nation, state, district, school, or grade of students.

Assimilation: Programming that is targeted for moving students from a minority culture into a majority culture.

Basic Interpersonal Communication Skills (BICS): The ability to converse or interact socially in everyday contexts.

Bilingual Syntax Measure (BSM): A language assessment of listening and speaking that is commonly used to identify English learners enrolled in public and public charter schools. It is used for students in preschool through Grade 12 and is available in English and Spanish.

Biliteracy: The ability to read and write in two languages proficiently. Generally, the person is equally proficient in both languages.

Cognitive Academic Language Proficiency (CALP): The level of language required for students to perform abstract and cognitively demanding classroom tasks without contextual supports such as gestures and the research of objects. Includes the language ability required for academic achievement.

Communicative Competence: The ability to use any form of language appropriate to the demands of social and academic situations. Includes linguistic knowledge, cultural knowledge, and interaction skills.

Content-Based ESL Instruction: A type of instruction for learning content while learning English. Generally, this type of instruction is planned and delivered by an ESL teacher or coplanned and codelivered by a general classroom and ESL teacher.

Content Standards: Brief statements that clearly state what students will know and be able to do. Should parallel the knowledge and skills that students are expected to learn and that are generally tied to school, district, state, or national standards or frameworks.

Coteaching: A teaching approach whereby an ESL and general classroom teacher share responsibility for coplanning and codelivering instruction in a general classroom.

Culture (also Cultural Way of Being): In this book, these terms are used to refer to two groups: (a) ELs and their families who are from diverse cultural experiences other than the dominant monolingual American English-speaking culture and (b) monolingual American English-speaking students, educators, parents, and community members. Drawing from Trueba, Guthrie, and Au (1981), these terms are used to describe "a form of communication with learned and shared, explicit and implicit rules for perceiving, believing, evaluating, and acting. . . . What people talk about and are specific about, such as traditional customs and laws, constitutes their overt or explicit culture. What they take for granted, or what exists beyond conscious awareness, is their implicit culture" (pp. 4–5).

Disaggregated Data: Generally refers to student subgroup performance on national, state, district, and/or school assessments.

Dual-Language Program: Also known as *two-way* or *developmental*, the goal is for students to develop language proficiency in two languages by receiving instruction in English and another language in a classroom that is usually comprised of half native English speakers and half native speakers of the other language.

English as a Second Language (ESL): A program of techniques, methodology, and special curriculum designed to teach English learners English language skills, including listening, speaking, reading, writing, study skills, content vocabulary, and cultural orientation. Instruction is usually in English with little use of a student's native language.

English Language Development (ELD): Instruction that is targeted for the learning of English. Is generally part of a program of instruction for English learners and usually includes all four language domains (listening, speaking, reading, and writing) as well as content vocabulary and supporting students' cultural orientation.

English Learner (EL): A student who has learned a language other than English during his or her primary years and is not able to do ordinary classroom work in English. The term EL is used interchangeably with limited

English-proficient (LEP) student, language-minority student, English language learner, and second language learner.

Equal Education Opportunities Act of 1974: Civil rights statute prohibiting states from denying equal access to educational opportunities to individuals based on race, color, sex, or national origin. Prohibits states from denying appropriate actions to overcome language barriers that impede equal participation of students in instructional programming.

ESL Pull-Out: A model of instruction whereby ESL is taught in a separate setting from the general education class.

ESL Push-In: A model of instruction whereby the ESL teacher coplans instruction with the general teacher and codelivers instruction in the general classroom using small groups and theme-based instruction.

Expediting Comprehension for English Language Learners Protocol (EOP): A research-based guide for lesson planning, delivery, and reflection that uses authentic assessment, tracks student progress, and includes a professional development component.

Formative Assessment: Typically occurs as part of lesson delivery as a means to check for understanding, provide students with immediate feedback, and make on-the-spot and future decisions regarding instruction. This type of assessment allows teachers to individualize instruction to meet the needs of learners.

Former Limited English Proficient (FLEP): A student who was formerly an English learner or limited English proficient who has achieved a level of English proficiency that approximates that of a native English speaker.

General Classroom: Mainstream classroom where subject matters are taught to English-fluent students and/or English learners of the same chronological age and/or grade.

High-Incidence Population (HIP): Generally refers to a large number of English learners from the same language group. In some districts, this might include 20 or more students.

Highly Effective: Phrase used when teachers have depth of knowledge for achieving student outcomes and when students are successful learners of English and content.

IDEA Proficiency Test (IPT): Language assessment of listening, speaking, reading, and writing that is commonly used to identify English learners enrolled in public and public charter schools. Includes tools for assessing students in preschool through Grade 12 and is available in English and Spanish.

Informed Parental Consent: Permission of a parent or legal guardian to enroll his or her child in an English learner program or the refusal to allow his or her child to enroll in such a program—after the parent has been provided with effective notice of program options and a district's recommendation for English language education programming.

Language Assessment Scale (LAS): Language assessment of listening, speaking, reading, and writing that is commonly used to identify English learners in public and public charter schools. Includes tools for assessing students in preschool through Grade 12 and is available in English and Spanish. Includes the Language Assessment Scale-Oral (LAS-0), Language Assessment Scale Reading/Writing (LAS R/W), and the more recent LAS Links, which includes assessments of all four language skills.

Language Dominance: A measurement comparing the proficiencies of two or more languages. Commonly used for describing the language that a student has more capacity in. This testing is often used during a special education evaluation to determine the language that students should be tested in to assess their academic, cognitive, and/or language performance.

Language-Minority Student: Used interchangeably with English learner and second language learner to refer to a student who has learned a language other than English during his or her primary years and is not able to do ordinary classroom work in English.

Limited English Proficient (LEP): Used interchangeably with English learner, language-minority student, and second language learner to refer to a student who has learned a language other than English during his or her primary years and is not able to do ordinary classroom work in English.

Low-Incidence Population (LIP): Generally, a small number of English learners from a particular language group.

Mission Statement: Tool for defining and sharing a district's goals and the ways in which progress toward achieving these goals will be measured. Commonly made available to the community at large.

Monitoring Charts: Means by which student performance is documented specifically and explicitly using a reliable and valid means for an intended purpose. Should be used repeatedly and systematically with a wide range of students, a specific set of timelines, and a clearly articulated process to ensure that the monitoring charts are doing what they are purported to do and ensure their effectiveness.

National Clearinghouse for Bilingual Education (NCBE): Provides information about bilingual education, ESL programs, Head Start, Title I, migrant education, and adult education programming, including an online library with information on topics such as demographics, characteristics of schools and programs, and news related to bilingual education.

National Clearinghouse for English Language Acquisition (NCELA): Collects, coordinates, and conveys a broad range of research and resources in support of an inclusive approach to high-quality education for English learners.

Native Language (L1): The first, native, or initial language learned by an English learner.

Newcomer Program: Primarily, separate self-contained program designed to meet the needs of newly arrived, mostly immigrant, beginning learners of English. Typically, students enroll in this kind of program before enrolling in general education classes with fluent speakers of English.

No Child Left Behind Act (NCLB): Federal mandate whose purpose is to improve the performance of K–12 schools by making states and schools more accountable for student progress and allowing parents more flexibility in choosing which schools their children will attend. Under NCLB, students, including English learners, must be tested annually to determine if their school has met Adequate Yearly Progress.

Peer Coaching: When two or more peers collaborate and observe each other's work to reflect on and improve their practice. Generally not tied to an evaluation system. Built on mutual trust and confidentiality to ensure a safe environment for professional growth.

Response to Intervention (RTI): Three-tiered approach for providing early identification and supports for students with learning and behavioral needs.

Tier 1: Research-based instruction that occurs in general classrooms and, in the case of English learners, in classes that have been designed for the purpose of learning English and/or a target language and content.

Tier 2: Intensive assistance as part of the general education classroom or, in the case of English learners, as part of a general English language education program.

Tier 3: Special education programming.

Rubric: Systematic scoring guideline or set of criteria for students, teachers, and others to use to assess performance based on a specific standard. Items are generally written in descending order, with the highest level at the top and lowest at the bottom. Generally includes descriptors of ability at each level of performance that are intended to be reliable, valid, and fair.

Second Language (L2): This term is used in different ways, including the second language learned chronologically, a language other than what is used in a student's home, and the target language being learned.

Second Language Learner: Used interchangeably with English learner, language-minority student, and limited-English-proficient student. Refers to a student who has learned a language other than English during his or her primary years and is not able to do ordinary classroom work in English.

Sheltered English Instruction: Instruction that is delivered in English with, but not always, clarification in a student's primary language that is meaningful and comprehensible. Often includes physical activities, visuals, manipulatives, and an environment in which students are provided with many context cues to make learning accessible.

Sheltered Instruction Observation Protocol (SIOP): Model of lesson planning and delivery for teaching content and language to English learners.

Structured English Instruction (also known as Structured English Immersion): Instructional approach used to make instruction in English meaningful and comprehensible. Generally, teachers of these classes have had training and/or possess credentials for teaching English learners (such as bilingual or ESL teachers) and are often fluent in a student's primary language.

Submersion Program: Program in which English learners are placed in a regular English-only program with little or no support services for learning English. Based on an unfounded theory that children will learn language naturally and be able to perform ordinary classwork in English with no additional supports.

Summative Assessment: Used after a unit of study is completed or a certain time period has occurred (e.g., the end of term) to determine how much learning has taken place. It is typical for grades to be assigned as part of a summative assessment.

Title VI of the Civil Rights Act of 1964: Prohibits discrimination based on race, color, or national origin by districts that receive federal financial assistance.

Title VII of the Elementary and Secondary Education Act (ESEA): Recognizes the unique needs of English learners. Established in 1968, it instituted a federal policy to assist educational agencies in serving English learners by authorizing the funding needed to do so. Also supports professional development and research.

Transitional Bilingual Education (TBE): Model of instruction whereby students receive instruction in their primary language in content areas until they are able to learn in English. Instruction in the primary language is reduced as students become more proficient in English, at which time no further instruction in the primary language is provided. Generally, also includes instruction in ESL.

WIDA Access Placement Test (W-APT): English language test that includes listening, speaking, reading, and writing components. Used by WIDA member states to identify English learners enrolled in public and public charter schools. Includes tools for assessing students in kindergarten through Grade 12.

WIDA Model for Kindergarten: English language test that is used to identify English learners ranging from 4.5 to 7 years of age.

Woodcock-Muñoz Language Survey–Revised (WMLS-R): Language assessment of listening, speaking, reading, and writing that is commonly used to identify English learners in public and public charter schools. Includes tools for assessing students in preschool through Grade 12 and is available in English and Spanish.

World-Class Instructional Design and Assessment (WIDA) Consortium: Consortium of 22 partner states: Alabama, Delaware, the District of Columbia, Georgia, Hawaii, Illinois, Kentucky, Maine, Mississippi, New Hampshire, New Jersey, New Mexico, North Carolina, North Dakota, Oklahoma, Pennsylvania, Rhode Island, South Dakota, Vermont, Virginia, Wisconsin, and Wyoming. Focuses on the planning and implementation of high-quality standards and equitable education for English learners. Provides six-level English language proficiency standards, assessment tools, research, professional development, and grant-funded projects.

Index

CORWIN

A SAGE Company

The Corwin logo—a raven striding across an open book—represents the union of courage and learning. Corwin is committed to improving education for all learners by publishing books and other professional development resources for those serving the field of PreK–12 education. By providing practical, hands-on materials, Corwin continues to carry out the promise of its motto: **"Helping Educators Do Their Work Better."**